BE A MAN!

SIX
PRINCIPLES
TO GROWING
AS A
MAN OF GOD

PASTOR GARY MORTARA

Be A Man!

Editing and Interior design: Casey Serafino-Lee

Cover design by: Mike Pine

*"So be strong, **show yourself a man**,*
and observe what the Lord your God requires:
Walk in his ways, and keep his decrees and commands,
his laws and requirements, as written in the Law of Moses,
so that you may prosper in all you do and wherever you go,...."

-1 Kings 2:2-3

When I was a child, I talked like a child,
I thought like a child, I reasoned like a child.
*When I **became a man,** I put childish ways behind me.*

1 Corinthians 13:11

DEDICATIONS

I dedicate this book to my precious family:

To my wife Tisha Christina of 20 years whose patience was proven through the process of my development: Thank you dear, I love you.

To my firstborn son, Michael David: you are and have been, a joy to our lives. My prayer is that the contents of this book will be a source of truth and blessing your whole life through. I love you son.

To my son Jonathan Daniel: Your quick wit and sweet spirit are a delight to mom and me. Remember how from infancy you have known the Holy scriptures. Continue in paths of righteousness for His name's sake. I love you son.

To my daughter and daddy's little princess, Liana Lee Alicia: You are the apple of my eye. Mom and I love you. I'm not always going to spoil you; well maybe just a little. I pray that not only will you live by the principles recorded in this book, which come from God's Word, but the man you choose to marry, will live by them also. I love you sweetie!

TABLE OF CONTENTS

ACKNOWLEDGMENTS

Special thanks to my secretary and dearest friend, Barbara Cabrera.
Thanks for all your support and encouragement.

Special thanks to Casey Serafino-Lee for all your hours of laboring with
the final editing of this book. I don't know what I would have done
without you.

Thanks to the Pastoral Staff at Faith Fellowship
for their encouragement to complete this book.

Special thanks to Mike Pine for designing the cover of this book.
You are awesome man!

Thanks to the I.M.F. Men's Group.
It was because of you that this book has become a reality!

And thanks to the entire family at Faith Fellowship Worship Center
in San Leandro California, for your love, prayers and support.
Your prayers carried me on eagles wings.

PREFACE

I began writing this book with the desire to help the men in our church develop and grow in the main areas of their lives which impact them on a day-to-day basis. As our church began to experience incredible growth, my counseling load also increased. I quickly realized that one hour appointments were just too long if I were to try and touch the lives of people and still find time for prayer and the deep study of God's Word. I had to find a way of dealing with people in a more timely manner, while still being effective.

Praying for our church and the lost who would come, along with preaching and teaching God's Word, were the number one priorities of my calling. The best way for any Pastor to effectively accomplish the task of shepherding and feeding the flock of God is through the systematic instruction of the Word of God on a weekly basis. Yet, I still wanted to maintain a level of "knowing the sheep" by sitting with and helping them in more isolated and private ways. In addition to weekly teaching, many people need, to one degree or another, some personal instruction.

As people continued coming in for "one-on-one" time, I realized that most of them were struggling in the same basic areas. I began keeping notes on index cards to see if my hunch was right; sure enough, people, especially men, were in principle, "missing it" in redundant ways.

My research shed some light on the issues and usually pointed to one of three things: most of them were either

1) not raised *with* their dads,

2) hadn't been trained *by* their dads, or

3) their dads were *poor examples* for them as they were growing up.

Now this didn't mean they were missing it in every area listed in this book, but usually in more than one. Some men needed help in just a couple of areas, and some men needed help in almost all of them. The unfortunate part was, most of the men coming in to see me were married, or soon to be married!

Although some men needed professional therapy due to earlier traumas and abuses, many of them simply needed basic training in Christian principles and living. It was a stark reality to talk to men who didn't know how to set up a budget, much less follow one. Other men had been steeped in sexual sin since their early teenage years and not only didn't feel a need to get help, but once they became a Christian, had no idea how to break this ungodly snare. This *was* and *is* affecting every area of their lives. Still others had no concept of how to actually lead a family with its built in responsibilities and heavy burdens.

Quite a number of men had not learned to control their emotions and words, and consequently have wounded relationships with both spouses and children. Some men, many actually, are newly saved and are just beginning their walk with Christ and haven't learned the blessing and discipline of a daily prayer life, Bible study, or the power of a close walk with God. Perhaps one of the saddest parts of all is that many men do not have a close friend with whom they can "buddy up" with for support. It is because of reasons such as these that I began writing this book.

I know that if you can embrace the principles and truths of Scripture contained herein, along with asking the Holy Spirit to broaden your understanding and application of them, you will grow and develop as a man of God. May the Lord richly bless you as you read this book.

Pastor Gary

INTRODUCTION

Welcome to the <u>Iron Men of Faith</u>® Ministry

It is with great pleasure and a deep sense of anticipation that we here at Faith Fellowship Foursquare Church in San Leandro, California, present to you a book for men. It is our desire to see you grow in the knowledge of our Lord and Savior Jesus Christ. We want to help bring fullness to your life by sharing truth with you from God's word, insight from His Spirit and examples from life's experiences. We realize that men come from a variety of different backgrounds, cultures, belief systems and habits of life, some of which may not line up with the Word of God. These attitudes and habits often cause conflict in our adult living which can rob the joy from our lives. Sometimes men are very strong in certain areas and weak in others.

In the following pages, I will give you principles from God's word on living a godly and victorious life as a man of God. As God himself gives you wisdom by His Spirit, and as you glean insights from this book, you will see progress from your efforts and they will be richly rewarded. Let's join our efforts and do it together.

This book will cover six key areas that make up the basic structure in being a man of God:

- •Accountable
- •Physical
- •Financial
- •Spiritual
- •Emotional
- •Mental

If you have been struggling or failing in any area as you desire to be a better husband, father, or man, this book will be a good start in the right direction. Take your time as you read through it. Read it often. Learn the principles and concepts. Practice new life behaviors. Be diligent. When you fall short, get back up. You will only lose if you stay down. Remember, we are at your side supporting you all the way.

For the cause of men,

Pastor Gary Mortara,
Iron Men of Faith (I.M.F.) Founder

CHAPTER ONE

Growing as a Man of God:

ACCOUNTABILITY

"Plans fail for lack of counsel, but with many advisers they succeed"
(Proverbs 15:22).

WHY DO I NEED TO BE ACCOUNTABLE TO SOMEONE?

A study was once done to see how much weight a horse could pull all by himself. As they gathered up different types of horses for the contest, the winning horse pulled an astounding 4,500 lbs. The second place horse pulled 4,400 lbs, which combined equals 8,900 lbs. However, when they teamed the two horses together they were able to pull over 12,000 lbs!

As we cover the five other foundational pillars of being a man of God, this section on accountability will aid us in bringing a stabilizing support for these pillars. Accountability is not a word or a concept that we easily adhere to. In this section we will uncover the fears, failures, and frustrations that cause us to avoid accountability. However, if the principles are applied, the rewards are well worth any discomfort. We will also see the *productivity* which comes from allowing ourselves to be open and transparent to other good men.

Alex Haley, who wrote the classic "Roots", has a picture in his office with this caption underneath it: **"If you ever see a turtle on top of a fencepost, you know he had help getting there".** That is what accountability and friendships are all about. Getting the most out of our lives with the help of a few good friends. Let's face it, **we all live in the same room in this world, the room for improvement!**

The strength of accountability is its ***built-in-ability*** which helps us to see things in our lives that we may not be aware of ordinarily. It seems to be especially difficult for men to open themselves up to friendships, counsel, correction, or anything else that may cause us to feel like "we can't do it by ourselves." Men, we aren't supposed to do it all by ourselves. In Ecclesiastes 4:9 it says, ***"Two are better than one, because they have a good return for their work."*** The fact is, men, we need each other. I have weaknesses and shortcomings, things I can't see from my perspective, habits that are too comfortable, and a host of other issues where I just need some good men around who can walk with me. It is suggested, implied, proven, and commanded in Scripture, that we are to be there to help each other. Sometimes I'm in need of help and counsel, and other times I am needed to give it. Maybe an illustration will help us see the importance of this Biblical truth.

I Am Your Brother

I remember going on an archery hunting trip high up in the Nevada mountains. My hunting partner, Brian Swinderman and I, had made the trip the previous year and had been shown the spot by an older gentleman who had hunted there in years gone by. We were climbing to the 10,000 ft. level, and we knew how physically demanding the hike was going to be. We were trying to get up to the deer's summer range which was in a remote area of intense geography.

Most of the deer in this particular summer range were mature bucks who hung out in stag parties. We had seen some impressive trophy animals on that first hunt, but due to the fact that it was our first real archery hunt, our skills didn't match those of the animals. Needless to say, we came home without the venison. Yet, the memories were outstanding.

The second year we went on this hunt, we asked another friend (we will call him Pete) to come along and join us. We had warned him a year in advance of the rigorous climb up the mountain. We had told him to get in shape or it wasn't going to be a whole lot of fun. As the time drew near to go, I could see that Pete hadn't taken us seriously and he was going to be suffering a little bit on this trip. He greatly underestimated just how steep and difficult the terrain really was. He was in for a surprise.

We drove the four wheel drive as far up the mountain as we could possibly go, parked the vehicle, loaded on our backpacks and began the arduous journey up the mountain. The mountain was just as steep as I remembered it, and our friend was failing quickly. Two hundred yards up the hill he was stopping to fix his pack and catch his breath. By the time Brian and I were to the top, Pete was nowhere to be seen. We waited about fifteen minutes, thinking he might crest the hill at any moment, but after a while it became evident that the hill had been too much for him.

My options were limited; do I let him suffer under his own lack of preparation, or do I go back and help my brother carry his burden? What would I want someone to do for me if my foolishness had gotten me in trouble? What would I need from a brother the next time I didn't properly prepare? I told Brian to go on ahead and set up camp while I went back and helped our friend out. Sure enough, there he was suffering under the load of his lack of preparation.

The Bible doesn't say to carry each other's burdens if it isn't their fault. It says "Carry each other's burdens, and in this way you will fulfill the law of Christ" (Galatians 6:2). We all have been unprepared or foolish; we all have been stubborn and have underestimated the requirements of the job. What if my friend's attitude had been, "**Just leave me alone; I got myself into this mess, and I'll get myself out***"? He might still be up on that mountain!* Even though a little embarrassed, he was very thankful that I had come back to help him. And by the way, I harvested my first Archery Buck on that trip.

As men, we need to be in each other's lives because our friends need us. By being there for someone, we are showing the love of God that resides within us. Just because "you have it all together" doesn't mean that you can look down on those of us who don't.

And if you __think__ you have it all together,
you may be in more need of help than any of us!

However, because *you probably have it together in some areas*, we do need you. Today you may be "making it up the mountain," but I promise you that there is a guy out there who really needs you to give him a helping hand. And what about the next time your burden is a little to heavy to carry? Will you let another brother help you? If you're too macho for that (which is foolish), you are keeping other men from obeying the Lord by not letting them help you! Think about it.

TELL ME THE TRUTH

Everybody loves to be encouraged and patted on the back. We all deserve accolades for different accomplishments that we have achieved. There are few things better than being told "You did a good job," or, "We couldn't have done it without you." Most of us come up way short in giving out compliments. I'm not talking so much about flattery, but rather seeing someone's effort and acknowledging it. Sometimes what is equally as important as encouragement and usually far more difficult is *speaking the truth in love when correction is needed.*

Proverbs 27:9 says, "...**the pleasantness of one's friend springs from his earnest counsel.**" The measure of a true friend is when he not only gives you encouragement and compliments, but he also gives you correction when everyone else may be talking behind your back or judging you. He is the kind of friend who is going to tell you the truth even if momentarily you might get bothered with him. He's a guy you can go to for an honest answer, someone who will "shoot straight" with you. He's your bud who can look at your situation objectively when you are too emotionally caught up in it to discern all the facts. He's the guy who gives you the other point of view, your wife's side of the argument, tells you what your boss may be thinking, or that something is hanging from your nose! He's not worried about losing your friendship because you trust him too much to be offended by his words of wisdom. We all need a friend like that. But where do you find one?

You may have been let down or even "burned" by a close friend in the past. I want you to know that in every relationship there is the possibility of being hurt. No, let me go so far as to say that *you will get hurt or let down to one degree or another.* That's the nature of any meaningful relationship. The relationships in which we don't allow people to hurt us are the ones where we remain distant and aloof.

For example, let's consider marriage. Because we love and care so much in a marriage relationship, this is where we get hurt most often. The key is not to **separate** but rather to **communicate**, to learn to forgive and to learn how to solve problems. There isn't anyone who is perfect and doesn't sin, far from it. Yet the investment made into a close friendship usually far outweighs the discomfort from the mistakes we all make.

My close friend, Vince Taylor, has had to overlook my faults, forgive my offenses, correct my mistakes, and live with my shortcomings. That's one reason why our friendship is so special. Remember the Scripture above, "the pleasantness of one's friend springs from his earnest counsel"? Our relationships are strengthened when we speak truth to each other. We can't run from meaningful relationships just because at times they are tough. That's part of the package. There are no perfect people, including you!

You might say, "I don't want to open myself to hurt or rejection."

We have to understand that no true friend wants to intentionally hurt us or fail to meet our expectations. It is because of shortcomings, mistakes, and other issues that we get let down. Sometimes our expectations of people are too high, and we set ourselves up to be disappointed. How would you ever practice the law of forgiveness if no one ever let you down? Working through those tough moments into healing is what makes for a deep and lasting relationship.

Maybe you can't see yourself being that kind of a friend. Maybe you perceive yourself as someone who is unable to give counsel and correction to another person. Listen to what Paul said in Romans 15:14, "**I myself am convinced, my brothers, that you yourselves are full of goodness, complete in knowledge *and competent to instruct one another*"** (emphasis mine). As we grow in the knowledge of God's Word and in life's experiences, we can trust the Holy Spirit to give us the wisdom we need to help others.

Let's ask God to put one or two guys into our lives who can be there for us and correct us. Let's also ask God to help us to be that kind of a friend. In the long run, we will be better men for it.

CONFRONTATION

There aren't too many of us who like being confronted and shown when we have been wrong or have made a mistake. It's usually uncomfortable for both parties - the person doing the confronting and the person being confronted. Who likes to be told "You missed it, brother"?

It goes against our pride. Our human nature contends, "I'm in charge, and I don't need you or anybody else telling me what to do." But the fact is, we all miss it from time to time. Proverbs 16:2 says, "**All a man's ways seem innocent to him, but motives are weighed by the Lord**." It isn't too difficult to feel right or justified in our actions, thoughts, or words, *when there is no one around to show us the other side.*

The Apostle Peter had just such a situation when he was in the city of Antioch. As a Jew, he traveled to the city of Antioch to help with this new gentile (non-Jewish) church. He made the journey with some other church leaders to strengthen and to fellowship with the new Gentile believers. Unfortunately he was found to be compromising in his conduct. He began treating the gentiles differently than he did the Jews. Even the other Apostles who were there were caught up in his racism and so they too joined in the hypocrisy. Sometimes we are blind to our own behavior.

As a Jew, Peter had firsthand experience in seeing the Gentiles come to Jesus Christ for salvation (see the story in Acts 10:1-48). He knew that all men - Jews and Gentiles - were *saved by faith in the LORD JESUS CHRIST*. The middle wall of separation between Jew and Gentile had been destroyed (Ephesians 2:14), and everyone had become a part of the family of God by faith in Jesus Christ (Galatians 3:26). But while he was in Antioch, some Jewish leaders came down from James (he was the leader of the Jewish Christian Church in Jerusalem and the half brother of Jesus) in Jerusalem to visit, and they saw Peter and the other Apostles associating with the Gentiles.

These Jewish men believed that a person had to also be circumcised in order to be a true Christian. Because Peter was afraid of these men, he started withdrawing from the Gentiles. He was compromising his integrity concerning what he knew to be the truth about the Gospel. Not only did he somehow justify his new actions, he was able to convince other men of God to do the same. When he ran into Paul, he was rebuked face to face in front of everyone. Paul said, **"Peter was clearly in the wrong"** (see Galatians 2:11-13). My question is: **"To whom was it clear?"** Certainly not to Peter. It was clear to Paul who was a good friend of Peter's but why wasn't it clear to Peter or the rest of the guys? *It is clear, that we don't always see clearly.* Is that clear?

Peter may not have liked the rebuke and most certainly must have been embarrassed by a public tongue lashing from the one guy he would have liked to have been complimented by. In the long run, however, he had more respect for Paul as a man who not only saw things that others didn't, *but had the guts to speak up when correction was needed.*

You and I might wonder if Paul used the proper method of rebuke when he did it publicly. Certainly there will be more times than not to take a brother aside alone and speak the truth in love. But remember, Peter had publicly led a whole group of leaders into open hypocrisy. Paul knew that what Peter was doing was damaging the truth of the gospel. By Peter making such an *open blunder*, Paul was quite right in making the rebuke just as open. Be careful of the public example you set. How would you have responded to Paul if you were clearly in the wrong? **How do you respond if you are corrected by someone**? Ask a friend how he thinks you react when you are corrected. You just might be surprised! Remember, we ourselves don't always see clearly. Keep this in mind as you continue on life's journey.

I once preached a series on the sin of David with Bathsheba. There is far more to this story than what is on the surface or can be realized in a casual reading. One thing the Scripture doesn't mention is, *someone challenging* the obvious actions which were wrong on the part of David. When someone is doing something that is undeniably a sin, we cannot sit idly by and say nothing! Someone has to stand up and ask, *"Why are you doing this?"*

Just because a person is a leader doesn't mean that they are above accountability. In fact, leaders are the ones who need it the most! When they make a mistake in judgment, it can affect a whole group of people. Unfortunately, leaders are the ones who usually don't want the accountability because pride breeds autonomy (Webster defines autonomy as 'a self-governing state' or more accurately 'self lawed'). Everyone needs a friend or a group of friends who can speak the truth into their lives when necessary.

We all remember the television evangelists who fell in the late 1980's. Both of them, by their own admittance said that they wanted "**yes men**" in their camp. By having people around us who won't challenge our wrong decisions, we are enabling ourselves to call all the shots, right or wrong. The more powerful you become, the less you think you need people telling you what to do. Success can breed arrogance. Arrogance and pride do not love God, they "**play God**"!

As stated above, we will all have times when we will be in the wrong and not realize it. Yet, it will be very clear to others. In the story of David and Bathsheba, we will see how this might have been avoided if someone had spoken up and simply asked, "*Why?*"

LUST OF THE EYES

Let's take a quick look at this account and see what could have been done differently. In 2 Samuel chapter 11, David saw a beautiful woman from his rooftop and sent someone to find out who she was. The man returned and told him that she was a *daughter of a man David knew and the wife of one of his best soldiers*. Even with this information, David proceeded with his adulterous plan. David sent messengers to bring her to him and they did.

Question: *Why didn't someone challenge David's sinful plan?* Why wasn't David concerned that someone might stop him? The answer lies in the fact that David didn't surround himself with men who had the courage to challenge or question him (after all, he was the king!). Granted, some of his best men were out at war, but the messengers whom he had sent to enquirer of the woman Bathsheba, didn't attempt to persuade him that this was wrong. Unfortunately, the whole nation would feel the repercussions of his choice.

After Bathsheba became pregnant, David sent for her husband Uriah to come and sleep with her to cover up his sin (2 Samuel 11:6). Bathsheba's husband, Uriah, was a man of honor, and while his fellow

23

soldiers were out on the battle field with the Ark of God, he wouldn't enjoy the pleasures of his home. The first night, Uriah slept on his own front porch (2 Samuel 11:9). The second night, David tried to get him drunk to blur his reasoning abilities; but again, he wouldn't budge (2 Samuel 11:13). David needed another plan to cover his sin. He sent a letter to Joab, the commander of his army. He told Joab to put Uriah on the front lines where the fighting was fiercest and to allow him to be killed. Joab did just what the king had ordered.

Why didn't Joab, the commander of the army, the king's friend, ask the king "why"? Uriah was one of David's mightiest and most loyal men. In fact, 1 Chronicles 11:41 says that out of several thousand soldiers, Uriah was in the top thirty. Why would the king want him killed? I can understand the loyalty of Joab to David, but what about the fact that Uriah had been loyal to both David and Joab?

Joab needed to ask, **"Why, why are we killing one of our best men who has served us so faithfully? I need an answer, David."** This should have been Joab's response.

As it turned out, no one challenged either of David's actions or motives but God was well aware of the entire situation, and Israel as a nation had to pay for it. If you get defensive when someone questions a decision that you have made, maybe you're getting defensive because..... you are wrong! You can get your own way if you are pushy enough, crafty enough, or want to be a lone ranger. But why be so foolish? It will end in misery. Proverbs 19:3 says, **"A man's own folly** (foolishness) **ruins his life, yet his heart rages at the Lord."** Not allowing yourself to be accountable to someone is foolish.

Proverbs 12:1 says, "**Whoever loves discipline loves knowledge, but he who hates correction is *stupid*"** (emphasis mine). Any man who wants to grow and develop in his character must be willing to listen to instruction and receive correction. There is not a person on this planet who is always right (except maybe in his own foolish mind) and never makes mistakes. Having a teachable heart and an understanding that we don't "**know it all**" places us on a path to greatness.

Now that we understand that we will be let down or even hurt in relationships, and that we don't always "see" so clearly, and that autonomy is *not* the path to greatness, we must begin to open up and seek out other male friendships. It is hard work. It is uncomfortable. Your view about things may be correct most of the time, but you must be accountable to other men. For as Scripture says, "**As iron sharpens iron, so one man sharpens another**" (Proverbs 27:17).

KEEPING OTHERS ACCOUNTABLE

The Scriptures not only give many illustrations about people who have been accountable, but they give examples of those who weren't. Proverbs 24:11-12 warns us, "**Rescue those being led away to death; hold back those staggering toward slaughter. If you say, "But we knew nothing about this," does not He who weighs the heart perceive it? Does not He who guards your life know it? Will He not repay**

each person according to what he has done?"

God is directly saying that He will hold us accountable for <u>not</u> attempting to hold others accountable when it is clear that they are in the wrong or are about to do something foolish. Question: If God is asking us to be available to others, isn't He then responsible to make sure that we can do the job? **What I'm saying is, you *can* be a good, close friend to other guys.** You *can* impart knowledge in certain areas where they might need correction or direction. You might only say to them, "I can see you are "missing it here", and I don't have the answer; but you should go talk to someone who has insight into these kinds of issues."

Your encouragement for them to seek help, *is* accountability. If you have the knowledge to keep them from making or continuing in a mistake, this is even better. You may be afraid and say to yourself, "I don't want to offend anyone" or worse yet, "I don't want to jeopardize a good friendship by speaking into his life in a corrective manner." When it came time to correct the Galatian church, Paul the apostle asked, "Have I now become your enemy by telling you the truth?" (Galatians 4:16). If being honest with our friends causes them to not want to be our friend, than it is not a friend that they want; we really aren't friends. As we said earlier, it's not just accolades and compliments that friends give to each other, but correction as well. Proverbs 17:10 says, "**A rebuke impresses a man of discernment more than a hundred lashes a fool.**" Here are three questions to ask ourselves when confronting a friend: 1) What is our motive for speaking into another man's life? 2) What is our method when speaking into another man's life? 3) What is the reason for not speaking into the life of another man?

Let's answer all of these questions. The answer to the first question, "what is our **motive** for speaking into another man's life," **should be that of love**. The reason for speaking up is that we don't want to see our friend do something that is wrong, sinful, foolish, or that will result in pain or loss.

The answer to the second question as to the "**method**" of confrontation is to speak the truth in love (it's important to remember why you are speaking to him). I'm not speaking to him to make myself look or feel better than him or to shoot down his self worth. Our motivation ought to be out of love and concern for him as a friend and a brother. 1 Peter 1:22 says, "...**have sincere love for your brothers, love one another deeply from a *pure* heart**" (emphasis mine). So my motive is love and my method is in love.

The third question, what is our reason for **not** speaking into his life, is just as powerful and significant. Usually the **reason** for **not** speaking into a friend's life is **fear**. Proverbs 29:25 says, "**Fear of man will prove to be a snare...**" If we are afraid that they will not like us, or afraid that others will think differently about us or that they will reject us, all of these and more will keep us from speaking up. 2 Timothy 1:7 says, "**For God hath not given us the spirit of fear**"...(KJV). *We should not be afraid of how **man** will respond if we **do** speak up, but rather how **God** will respond if we **don't!***

Another reason why we may not speak up is, a feeling that it is "not our place". If we are friends, and it's not our place, then whose place is it? Please understand, there are important ingredients to correcting a friend, such as timing, making sure that we have the facts right, do we

27

know both sides of the argument, and deciding whether we should be the ones to confront them or should we send someone else instead. Above all, remember that love must be the motive. All these things and more need to be taken into account before we go to correct a brother.

Honestly, the first step is to go to prayer and ask the Lord, "what, when, why, and how," before we approach the person. The story of Nathan and David is a classic example. After David had committed adultery and then murder, the Lord sent Nathan to David with a convicting illustration of David's sin. Not only was it unequivocally wrong, but it was the kind of sin for which there was absolutely no excuse! David had many wives and the Lord had blessed him in many ways and had told David he would have blessed him with even more if he just asked (2 Samuel 12:8). But David had taken Uriah's *one and only wife* and then had Uriah murdered.

The point here is that Nathan did what the Lord had told him to do and said what the Lord had told him to say. What David did with the information was between David and God. Nathan accomplished his mission; he spoke into a leader's life without concern for what David might have done to him. We are commanded by the Lord to show a brother the error of his way (James 5:20). In fact, in the thirty-third chapter of Ezekiel in verses 1-9, God told Ezekiel that if he didn't speak out to dissuade a man from his evil way, the man would die for his sin and God would hold Ezekiel accountable. If he did speak out and the man didn't turn from his way, he would die; but Ezekiel would not be held accountable.

MAKING CHANGES THAT LAST

One of the most important times of needing a friend or being one, is when we are implementing Godly changes in our lives. Once changes have begun, "staying on track" is one of the most difficult parts of being successful. As we begin acting in new ways, our patterns of thinking will need to be altered as well. Looking at things in a positive way rather than from a negative frame of mind, is a major key in making profitable changes. *This is where a buddy plays the most important role. He must be consistent in checking in on you, assuring that you're still on track. He must look you right in the eyes and ask you, "How are you doing?"*

It will be too easy to slip back into those familiar old patterns of doing things that feel comfortable. Having a buddy who is going to ask the tough questions will help us to continue moving forward. I cannot overemphasize the importance of follow-up. All the other principles listed above can be done right; but if you don't follow up for weeks or months after, most people will slip right back into those negative patterns. Now is the time to be a friend. To be a friend, you have to act like one. Smile, ask questions (people love to talk about themselves), listen, do something special for them. Be realistic regarding how much time you or the other guy can give to the friendship, and give the relationship time to develop. Philippians 2:4 says, "**Each of you should look not only to your own interests, but also to the interests of others.**"

What About My Unsaved Buddies?

What do you do about unsaved buddies who still want to be friends? I myself remember the struggle of wanting to live my life for Jesus and yet not lose relationship with my unsaved friends. These are guys that I had grown up with or had developed close relationships with over the years that still wanted to "hang" with me but wanted me to still be the same 'old Gary'. I had to make a decision about my friends. Was I strong enough as a Christian to not let their influence sway me back to old patterns? If not, I would need more time to grow and mature before I could just hang out with them. On the other hand, who was going to evangelize them if I wasn't ready? So the question remained, "Who was going to out-influence whom"? If they could influence me back to ungodly things, then it wasn't time for me to just "chill" with them. Is there a balance in serving Jesus and still maintaining old friendships, or is it simply "cut-them-off" and go on with the Lord?

If you know in your heart that you will probably stumble backwards if you spend time with old friends, than now isn't the time for you to do that. You can still pray for them, ask them to church or to a men's retreat or function. But simply going back to old haunts when you know you are not ready may do more damage than good. If they see you weaken in your convictions by cussing, whistling at women, telling jokes, etc. they will see it for what it is, hypocrisy. However, if you know you are grounded in the Lord and have no desire of going back to those things, you may be the one person who can reach them with the gospel. Pray about it and talk to your wife or pastor and most of all, be honest with yourself.

In Conclusion

First of all, we all need friends who are close enough to us to be honest with us and speak the truth in love. Second, there will be times when we will be let down or hurt; but that is a part of any friendship. Third, the fact is, I need you, and you need me. God created us to be social people. He did not call us to live isolated lives on an island. Finally, I realize that sometimes my burden may feel too heavy for me, and I'll need someone to come along and help me, and at other times, I'll need to be there to help a brother carry his load. One thing is for sure: I don't know it all, and neither do you. In the areas where I am not too knowledgeable and you are, you will need to help me. Conversely, in the areas where you may be lacking and I may be strong, I can help you.

We definitely need each other. We are going to ask you to "step out of your comfort zone" and find a godly confidant, someone with whom you can begin to establish a growing relationship with. We all need people to laugh and have fun with! Find a guy who shares the same interests as you and begin there. I think you'll be amazed at how "cool" some guys really are. It takes time to develop a relationship. The more time you spend with a guy over the next year, the more comfortable you will be to open your life and your heart to him.

As you ask the Lord for help, He will send the right person your way. It may not happen today, but then again, maybe it will. You'll never know unless you step out and try. Remember, our church will be here to help you. Together we will make a powerful team.

CHAPTER TWO

Growing as a Man of God:

THE PHYSICAL SIDE

"After all, no one ever hated his own body, but he feeds and cares for it, just as Christ does the church—for we are members of his body." **Ephesians 5:29-30**

For many people, the physical side of a man may seem to be the least important. But remember, the physical side of a man is that which acts out what is in the heart and mind. Every physical act is simply a response from what is in the heart or mind of an individual. Controlling how our bodies act or respond is accomplished by controlling our desires, thoughts, and emotions. We have been given a body, a flesh and blood "tent" in which the real us is housed and we are responsible for the upkeep and maintenance of our bodies. The Bible says to those who are Christians, "**Do you not know that your body is a temple of the Holy Spirit, who is in you, whom you have received from God? You are not your own...**" (1 Corinthians. 6:19).

In the last twenty years, we have seen an increase in people's awareness concerning health and diet. With increased knowledge in the medical field, better health care programs, and updated information concerning a health conscious diet, the life span of people in America has increased. People who were at one time addicted to *not* exercising and working out, have now become those who are enamored with looking and feeling good.

BECOMING AND STAYING PHYSICALLY FIT

I want to take a few moments and mention the wisdom of properly feeding and caring for our physical bodies. In the Old Testament God gave his people dietary laws to follow. These were not given simply to add to all the other laws that God had already given; they each had a distinct purpose. Contemporary doctors and scientists have discovered the wisdom in these seemingly restrictive laws of God. Like a highly efficient engine, the human body runs best and lasts longer when it is given the proper fuel.

A consistent diet of the earth's natural foods is the best fuel for our bodies. Fruits, vegetables, nuts, grains, and moderate amounts of fish and poultry are the most nutritious. Foods that keep most of their natural nutrients help keep the body strong and clear of "clogs." It has even been proven that people who have contracted cancer have seen incredible improvements by drastically changing their diets.

High doses of real fruit and vegetable juices such as carrot juice and cranberry juice have been greatly effective in curbing or even curing cancer and other diseases. The "fast foods" that Americans take in have proven to be the cause of the massive numbers of heart disease and many types of cancer.

Dr. Bradley Gascoigne, a Kaiser Hospital pediatrician, recommends a healthier diet in his book <u>Smart Ways to Stay Young and Healthy</u>. Here is a list that he compiled for a healthier life:

"At least once a week, have legumes as your main source of protein; legumes include Lima beans, kidney   beans, navy beans, pinto beans, soybeans, peanuts (and peanut butter), lentils, split peas, black-eyed peas,   and chickpeas.

1) Include complex carbohydrates (whole grains, pastas, breads, cereals, and potatoes) in your diet; avoid simple sugar.
2) Include a daily source of fiber.
3) Cut back on fat, especially animal fat and saturated fats. Omega-3 oils found in salmon, tuna, sardines, and mackerel probably protect us from heart disease, but animal fats, which are found in meats and dairy products, increase our risk of heart disease.
4) Get enough iron (found in lean meats, beans, fish, whole-grain products, and iron-enriched cereals), which is important for children and menstruating women.
5) Avoid salt and too much sodium if you have high blood pressure and are salt sensitive; check with your physician.
6) Consider Tabasco® sauce as a substitute for salt.
7) Include at least 800 mg. of calcium in your daily diet.
8) Eat regular breakfasts, which enhance morning performance.
9) Avoid eating large dinners, which put on extra weight.
10) Include daily sources of Vitamin A, which contains beta carotene and which is considered protective against cancer, and is found in carrots, sweet potatoes, peaches, apricots, cantaloupes, spinach, squash and papaya.
11) Avoid cancer-causing substances that may be produced by frying, broiling or barbecuing chicken, meat, and fish; instead try to microwave, stew, boil or poach meats that you eat.
12) Limit caffeine intake to less than four cups of coffee per day.
13) Probably the soundest and simplest dietary advice these days is: *include five servings of fruits and vegetables in your daily diet...* and you will avoid many of the health risks above."

As stewards of these awesome "machines" in which God has given us to live in, we must consider what treatment we are giving them by way of our diet. If you are anything like me, changing your diet can feel like a massive undertaking! But, it can be done. Think about it; do you want to live the last 10 or 15 years of your life in bad or poor health, a burden to your children or grandchildren, and unable to enjoy your retirement?

Along with proper diet, our bodies must be exercised regularly to be kept in good working order. As a pastor, I know how easy it is to be so busy and fatigued that it seems almost impossible to find time to work out. However, I can't "buy into this lie". Working more with my mind than my body from behind a desk, I have trained myself to schedule in blocks of time to work my muscles and cardiovascular system. I have maintained my weight and body structure which I had when I was competing as an athlete back in my teens and early twenties. I make it a priority of life.

We currently have three services on Sunday morning (we used to have four services until the building of our new larger sanctuary). Instead of feeling more tired, I feel rejuvenated and awake. Working out by exercising my body allows me the stamina to accomplish this work for the Lord. I want to look and feel the best I can so as to get the most out of my life. I believe God demands it and I deserve it. How about you?

Consider purchasing some weights or a stair stepper for your office or home, and work out while watching a movie, the news, or listening to a tape. If you can do this at least two or three times a week, you will see a vast difference in your energy level. Many people in our church have joined a local gym and work out as "partners" to help motivate each other.

We have even started up a **First Place**[1] Bible-study and weight-loss class. As a matter of fact, it has been so successful that we are beginning a **co-ed** First Place class. The ladies are seeing remarkable results, and the men have noticed too!

Resting your body is equally as important. It has been said that America is run by tired men. God not only establishes dietary laws but also laws for exercise and rest. For six days people were to work. This was good hard physical labor. This was their "gym." You can bet that with the diet God had given them, and working hard six days a week, they were physically fit. (Many of them lived into their nineties and even hundreds, at a time when very little medicine had been discovered). Then on the seventh day they were to rest. They could do no work at all!

God created the physical body, and He knows best what sustains it. God gives man the breath of life, and God can demand the life of anyone, anytime he wants. However, if His laws are followed, even by unbelievers, the physical body can enjoy the opportunity for good health and long life.

When you read the story of Caleb in the Old Testament found in the book of Joshua chapter 14:6-11, his comment was that now at 85 years of age, he was just as strong and vigorous as he was when he was 45! Here is why I believe he could say this; **He obeyed God's Word.** Proverbs 4:20-22 says, "My son, pay attention to what I say; listen closely to my words. Do not let them out of your sight, keep them within your heart; **for they are life to those who find them and health to a man's whole body**." Caleb kept all of the dietary laws of a nutritious diet. He

---

[1]   First Place is a Christ–centered health program that produces a well-balanced life through spiritual, emotional, mental and physical well being.

37

also rested his body on a regular basis.

Only God knows the number of days He has set for us to live, but I want to live at least as many as He has in mind for me! Not properly feeding, exercising, or resting the body has cause many people to not live out their full life span. In addition, drug, alcohol, or tobacco addictions will almost certainly cut your life short. Make a decision today to eat right, exercise, and rest your body. It's the only one you have, for now!

STAYING FIT

For the Christian, the physical side of our responsibility goes a little deeper than exercise and diet. Let's look at the responsibility of being in control of the **actions** of our bodies. Paul the Apostle, who wrote most of the New Testament, said to his young colleague Timothy, "**For physical training is of some value, but godliness has value for all things, holding promise for both the present life and the life to come**" (1 Timothy 4:8). Timothy was a young man, probably in his early thirties, living in a sports oriented culture much like our own. He had most likely been some sort of athlete growing up, for Paul speaks on a few occasions with athletic illustrations. Here iws the wisdom of what Paul was saying, "It's okay to work out and stay in shape, eat right and get enough sleep and to feel good about yourself; but all of that is only good for so long. If it were a choice between being in shape or living Godly, choose living Godly. But God is saying you can do both; be in shape and live Godly".

There have been many people who were in great shape and yet

have prematurely died because of a disease. Others have been killed in accidents, and others have been murdered. And even if you aren't in great physical shape, living as a real Christian in righteousness and true holiness will benefit you both now and for all eternity." We will all have new bodies in eternity without the fear of sickness, or aging, let alone weight gain! Paul was letting Timothy know that how he used his body (whether in righteousness or for sinful indulgences) would affect his eternal perspective. Go ahead and serve God and allow yourself the blessing of being in shape while you do.

Addicted to Nothing

In the building of the physical side of a man, we want to help you with addictions and behaviors that immobilize you in your development as a complete man of God. Your integrity will always be questioned and it will be difficult, if not impossible, for a wife and family to want to follow your leadership if areas of your life are out of control! The great news is that you really don't have to be addicted to anything! You really don't have to live your life wishing you could be free. In Christ Jesus, you can be free!

In Christ Jesus there is power provided by the Holy Spirit to help you conquer every area of your life. This is one of the reasons why Jesus came to earth, to set the captive free (Luke 4:18). Before you became a Christian (if you've already made that decision) you were under Satan's power. You were a part of his kingdom, being ruled and mastered by Him

(Ephesians 2:2; Acts 26:18). Now however, you are part of another kingdom; God's. It is the *will of God* for you to walk in newness of life, and this includes having your mind changed to think in new patterns.

It is His will that you begin to lead a life in which you understand, **not only why** you have lived the way *you* have, *but* **why others live the way** *they* **do**. You will be able to help them become victorious as they seek to please God in everything they do. Being connected to a good Bible-teaching church will help you to keep growing in each area.

We all know the "**high cost of low living**". Many men have ship-wrecked their reputation and good name by not controlling how they have conducted themselves. As Christian men who have the Holy Spirit, we are not to allow our bodies to be instruments of sinful or unhealthy habits. Romans 6:11-14 says, "**In the same way, count yourselves dead to sin but alive to God in Christ Jesus. Therefore do not let sin reign in your mortal body so that you obey its evil desires. Do not offer the parts of your body to sin, as instruments of wickedness, but rather offer yourselves to God, as those who have been brought from death to life; and offer the parts of your body to him as instruments of righteousness. For sin shall not be your master, because you are not under law, but under grace.**" What a powerful passage of scripture. Rather than being a slave to what once mastered us, we are to conduct ourselves in such a way that the world looks up to us, not down upon us. *We are to be Spirit-led and Spirit-controlled.*

As a man with trials just like you, I too at one time tasted most of the "flavors" this world has to offer, and I'm letting you know that a life lived serving the Lord is a real life. The Christian life is the most fulfilling life there is! Yes, at times it is difficult; but living without Him is ludicrous.

Addictions can come in many different packages. The most obvious addictions are alcohol, drugs, pornography, tobacco, food, and work. However, there are many subtle kinds of addictions; things such as hobbies, soda pop, T.V., sports, spending, clothes, etc. In 1 Corinthians 6:12, Paul says, *"Everything is permissible for me – but not everything is beneficial. Everything is permissible for me – but I will not be mastered by anything"*. Anything which is illegal, mind altering, or is controlling behavior (this includes prescription drugs) is an addiction. Ephesians 5:18 says, **"Do not be drunk with wine which leads to debauchery (sensual pleasure) but be filled with the Spirit"**. What Paul was saying is **"don't be controlled or intoxicated by anything except the Holy Spirit"**.

Temptation: Stay Away!

Ephesians 5:3

"But among you there must not even be a hint of sexual immorality, or of any kind of impurity, or of greed, because these are improper for God's holy people."

As men of God, we have one master, and He is the Lord Jesus

41

Christ. God has designed our bodies with **needs** and **desires** which we are required to manage and maintain in a way that is honorable and consistent with who we are in Christ. God, the Holy Spirit, not only teaches us but also gives us the power to maintain the proper perspective and heart attitude so that all inappropriate desires and drives are kept in subjection. Because we are held responsible for the actions our bodies take, this makes it clear that we must carefully monitor what attracts or entices us.

The great statement by our Lord, "**The spirit is willing but the body is weak**" (Matthew 26:41) is all so true anytime *we allow ourselves* to be tempted beyond what we are able to overcome. Someone once said, " Every man must know his limitations." For me this means, "**if something has the potential of taking over my life or conduct by way of its powerful influence, I must exercise wisdom and stay away from it.**" God has promised that He would not allow us to be tempted beyond that which we are able to overcome; and whenever there is such a situation, He has also promised to provide a way of escape (see 1 Corinthians 10:13-14).

However, let me state right here that even though God will not allow us to be placed in a situation which is beyond our ability to withstand, so many times **we place ourselves in situations which are too much for us to handle!**

The classic recorded story of Joseph being tempted by the wife of his employer is a case in point (Genesis 39). He was simply doing his best to serve the Lord by serving his boss. Potiphar's wife took notice of his physical attributes and desired his company under the covers. God had *allowed* the temptation at this level because He knew the man who was being tempted. God did not remove Joseph from the situation but rather had him see the eternal consequences (and also the front door of the house)! Joseph's victory was due to his ability to *"SEE and THINK"* rather than *"FEEL and FALL!"*

Let's consider the difference between God allowing temptations to come our way and our own foolishness of "playing with fire and getting severely burned." If God won't let us be tempted beyond what we are able to overcome, why do **we** place ourselves in situations that will be too much for us? God knows that we live in a fallen and sin-filled world - a world that we have been **a** *part of* and *partakers of.* Things in this world still have a possibility of leading us astray if we are not wise concerning our humanness. As in the case of Joseph, the world "sets us up for a fall." You and I both know the things that tempt us. You can be sure that they will continue to cross our paths, but, we really don't have to give in; we really don't!

With Joseph, God could have prevented the whole thing by striking Potiphar's wife dead, sending a timely earthquake, or a host of other "acts of God." God didn't create the temptation, but He did allow it. The way of escape was Joseph's conscience (what he knew was right and wrong), his fear of God, and a choice. There will always be something or someone to lead you astray. You must determine how you will handle the situation before it arrives.

Stephen Covey in his book <u>Principle Centered Leadership</u> said, "Just as the education of nerve and sinew is vital to the athlete, and education of the mind is vital to the scholar, education of the conscience is vital to primary greatness. Training the conscience, however, requires even more discipline. It requires honest living, reading inspiring literature, and thinking noble thoughts. Just as junk food and a lack of exercise can ruin an athlete's condition, things that are obscene, crude, or pornographic can breed an inner darkness that numbs our highest sensibilities and substitutes the *social conscience* of, 'Will I be found out?' for the *natural conscience* of, 'What is right and wrong?'"

WHAT IF?

Let's contrast the **true** story of Joseph with a *fictitious, rewritten, story of Joseph*. Joseph was attracted to his employer's wife. He liked being around her, the way she smelled, looked, and how she made him feel (remember, this is fictitious). Instead of refusing to be with her, he made it a point to be in places where he knew she would be. He knew she was attracted to him and this made it even more enticing. When finally she made her move, "**All at once he followed her like an ox going to the slaughter, like a deer stepping into a noose till an arrow pierces his liver, like a bird darting into a snare, little knowing it will cost him his life.**" (see Proverbs 7:22-27). The difference lies in how we place ourselves in vulnerable situations that we know can weaken us to the point of giving in to temptation. *You must flee now!*

Whatever your weakness might be, sex, drugs, alcohol, gambling, etc, make up your mind *before* you ever get into temptation that you will flee at the very appearance of evil. Also, whenever you see the possibility of a temptation directly ahead of you, don't wait for it to come upon you to try to be strong, plan your escape right now! We both know that there is a point of no return.

An example might be, if you are making a commitment to stop drinking and you are going to a wedding reception where there will be alcohol, have a friend or your spouse keep you accountable. Don't see this as a light thing. Don't fool yourself by saying, "I can handle it". Let them help. It doesn't mean you are weak; it means you are smart!

Another approach might be to look back at the times when you have fallen in this area. Is "giving in" brought on by fatigue, depression, anger, or a sense of feeling strong or good? Begin to prepare yourself now by having a plan of attack against it. The same goes for drug addictions, tobacco, or whatever tempts you.

James 1:13-15, tells us why we sin. **"When tempted, no one should say, 'God is tempting me.' For God cannot be tempted by evil, nor does He tempt anyone; but each one is tempted when, by his own evil desire, he is dragged away and enticed. Then, after desire has conceived, it gives birth to sin; and sin, when it is full-grown, gives birth to death."** When we sin, it is simply *us* giving in to that which *we* desire!

If you wanted to tempt me to overeat, you wouldn't serve me a large portion of liver and onions. It does nothing for me. I wouldn't be tempted by it in the least. But you place before me a thick, juicy, rib-eye steak, cooked medium well, with mushrooms and corn on the cob, I would need all my strength and God's too not to be a glutton.

Hebrews 12:1 says, "...**let us throw off everything that hinders and the sin that so easily entangles...**" Also, Romans 12:1 says "**Therefore, I urge you, brothers, in view of God's mercy, to offer your bodies as living sacrifices, holy and pleasing to God-this is your spiritual act of worship.**" Romans 6:11 instructs us to "**Count yourselves dead to sin but alive to God in Christ Jesus.**"

SEXUAL SIN

Probably one of the biggest addictions we men face is that of sexual things; pornography in particular. I will go so far as to say that most every man who is "**not saved**" in this country dabbles at some level in pornographic material. They either pick up a magazine filled with photographs of naked women, consistently view "R" or "X" rated movies, lust after a seductively dressed female, visit prostitutes or adult book stores, or entertain sinful sexual fantasies with an end result of self-gratification. Now before we go judging them, remember, **these are the men that Jesus came to save;** sinners, of all kinds. They come to salvation with the world's baggage dragging behind them. It is our job as Christian men to show them the path to freedom.

When a man comes to salvation and is born-again, it does not mean that every bad habit or all his sinful conduct instantly vanishes. It can, but it doesn't always happen that quickly. It comes down to a willingness to change as the Holy Spirit empowers and teaches us how. Let me give you a positive example of a case where change came quickly by making a difficult decision.

Before I knew that God was calling me into the ministry, I was working hard at becoming a professional golfer. At age 15, I had thrown my arm out chasing a baseball career which had been my dream and passion. I missed out on playing high school baseball due to the injury and thought I would never get to play ball again. At age 19, my arm strength returned and in just 9 months of training, I was still good enough to get a try out with the San Francisco Giants. After trying out for a short period with the Giants, I turned to professional golf. Golf was the career I was pursuing when I gave my life to Christ at age 22.

On Tuesday, the second day of my salvation (I became a Christian on Monday, November 17, 1980), I began a graveyard shift working at a gas station so I could work on my golf game during the day. I was turning pro in a short while and the job enabled me to practice every day and have some "walking around" money. The downside was that there was a stack of "girlie" magazines that were kept inside the gas station by the other employees.

Like other men in the world, up until the day I became a Christian I thought it no big deal to just pick up a magazine and look through it, allowing my mind to wonder and imagine every crude thought it desired with no effort towards control on my part. But now I had confessed Jesus as Lord and I knew that He was calling me to a new lifestyle. The first night at work I was faced with a decision that would "**set the course**" concerning this area of my life. Would I pick up a magazine and gaze at it's alluring contents, or would I walk in obedience to the Spirit of God and destroy this ungodly bondage?

The choice I made that first night **not to look** has helped me stand for 24 years against this "tentacle-like" passion. In three months of working at that establishment, I never once looked at a magazine, **not even once.** That victory was far greater than just defeating pornography. It taught me the truth of Philippians 4:13; "**I can do all things through Christ which strengtheneth me**" (KJV). It gave me faith and confidence that I could stand victorious in other areas of my life as well. The same goes for you too!

If you are mentally or physically addicted to any inappropriate sexual behavior (or any kind of habit), you must make a choice that will lead you to freedom. You must stop this sin and seek Godly help. This is the will of God for your life! (see both 1 Thessalonians 4:3-7 and 1 Corinthians 6:9-10). Don't keep it hidden, or worse yet, justify it by some weird philosophy that says, " **I'm not really addicted,**" or, " **God gave me these drives,**" or whatever other foolish rational that you can come up with. *These are lies!*

Believing these lies will only cause you to continue on in your sin and bondage and this is a devilish deception. This is the world's perspective, not God's. Jesus said, "**But I tell you that anyone who looks at a woman lustfully has already committed adultery with her in his heart.**" (Matthew 5:28). Most of our Christian battles are **not** fought and won in a single encounter. *It is a life of continual victories.* That first night of saying "no" to the magazines broke a bondage in me that has made it easier as a way of life for me to say no to other tempting situations in my life.

A Mouse in my House

One day I noticed a mouse running and hiding in our garage. There was a 1-2 inch gap under the garage door leading to the side yard of our house. I hadn't thought much of it before that, but now having observed this little critter running and hiding under my hunting gear, he had my attention. I decided on a plan of attack. I quickly searched out some old mouse traps stored in the junk box and analyzed the best set-up for my ambush. My bait of choice - good old fashioned peanut butter! They can't resist it.

That first night, I placed the bait in a strategic corner of the garage. I gently placed it in the center of the mouse's intended path of travel and went to sleep just knowing he had lived his last night. In the morning I couldn't wait to get up and see the trophy I had caught. To my surprise, he wasn't there, and to make matters worse, neither was the peanut butter! He had eaten all the peanut butter without tripping the trap. Now I was ticked. Tonight, he would die. Or so I thought.

The next night the same thing happened again, and the next night again, and then again. This mouse was eating up my son's lunch, and I had nothing to show for it. I needed to find out the problem. My tiny little friend was playing with me. What he didn't realize was, I figured out how he was getting away with it. When I grabbed the mousetrap out of the junk box, it had been there for a couple of years and the spring was so tight it wouldn't release without a lot of pressure. He would simply lick off the peanut butter very lightly and finish his free meal. Boy was he in for a surprise. I went down to the store and purchased a brand new set of mousetraps and once again that night set it out in the place. That night the mouse had his last meal of my son's peanut butter.

What happened to that mouse is what happens to us on a regular basis. We keep playing with sexual temptation and getting away with it, and we forget about the danger that can follow. We think it's O.K. Each night that mouse got away with the peanut butter it gave him more confidence that the next time he could get away with it. By the fifth night he was simply following his old pattern. The problem was, now the real trap had been set. Unfortunately, this confidence of "not being caught" was the very thing that got him caught. Finally the new trap released and ended his free pleasure.

This sounds almost identical to the story of Samson with Delilah. Each night he kept playing with sin and messing with Delilah's mind, thinking he was getting away with it. In reality however, he was only moving closer to his impending doom. We he finally told her the truth he was so sure that nothing was going to happen because nothing had ever happened, it cost him sight and eventually his life. Remember, like with Samson, sin blinds, sin grinds, and sin binds. Guys, right now is the time to get away from this sin. As evangelist Ravi Zacharias has said, "It is better to shun the bait then to struggle in the snare!"

What pornography does to a person

When a man gets involved in pornographic materials, things such as magazines, videos, movies, internet sites, or visiting clubs and strip bars, they begin to believe this is the way all women behave. They forget these are actors playing a part for the sake of money. They "actors" are playing on the sexual weaknesses of human beings, and they themselves are slaves to sin. Men are watching women easily give in to the advances of men they just meet, or, actually initiating sexual behavior towards the men making facial expressions and saying seductive and provocative things. They think this is what all women want and therefore see them only as sex objects to fulfill the male sex drive. This leads to a perverted mindset and perpetuates a view of women that isn't at all accurate.

From this perverted mindset comes an **inability** to see the next woman that they date, or their spouse, in a loving and wholesome way. The worse part is that it breeds a deep inner lack of trust towards their girlfriend or spouse because "all women are this way". When a man who is steeped in pornography has sexual relations with his wife, he sees her as acting just like the women in the video or the movie and thinks she is that easy for every man. He cannot trust her since he thinks this is the way she is; all based on the images in his mind from the pornography. They see everything through the eyes of the pornography they have continually

51

observed. They become accusatory of them and can never trust them properly, all because they have seen women in these "acting roles".

Anytime another man is around her, or she is late coming home, he can't help but think she must be out doing something. On top of that, they then want their spouses to perform some of the more nasty things in sex which they have watched in the pornography and when the spouse doesn't feel comfortable with that, they become upset. They begin demanding sexual favors based on what they think is "normal". This is unfair and is damaging to the marriage relationship. Therefore, it is quite clear that absolutely nothing good comes out of watching pornography or sexually graphic material. In addition, we must remember, that people who are involved in pornographic behavior are sinners who are lost and in need of God's salvation which comes through faith in Jesus Christ. They desperately need Jesus, and yet, men are paying money to keep them steeped in their sin. We know this is not the will of God.

STEPS TO VICTORY

Here is a 5 step outline that may help in victorious Christian living. As with any area of life which is a problem, you must **first** acknowledge that it is a problem. The **second** step is to make up your mind that you really want to stop. This is where most guys miss it. In their hearts they really aren't ready to quit. The **third** step is believe that you have the ability to stop and conquer this problem with the help of the Holy Spirit. Step **four**, requires that you stay accountable to another man who will walk with you. Finally, the **fifth** step to victory is realizing that **it will be a battle for the very life of you**. Read these steps over one or two times.

God has destined for both you and me to overcome sin in every area of our lives. There will be times when we seem to be doing well. Then out of nowhere, something happens that triggers these all too familiar desires to go back and surrender to those octopus-like tentacles of sin that want to destroy us.

Guys ask me all the time, "how do you conquer looking at other women?" I do not want to give some simple Christian platitude as though you'll never have another battle with it again. In our day and age it seems to be paraded in front of us without any shame or embarrassment. Women dress in provocative ways *just so we will look*. They seem to be saying, **"Look if you like, I know I look good. Don't you wish you could touch? If you play your cards right big boy, maybe I'll let you. Oh, and if you're married, it makes it all the more fun."** It's like we've been thrown into the lion's den!

God made men visual beings. We are "turned on" by sight. But please let me remind you that sin is an issue of the heart! The eyes are the gateway to the soul, and if your heart is full of lust, your eyes will look until they find what the heart is searching for. Because sexual sin has always been around, God said, **"But since there is so much immorality, each man should have his own wife, and each woman her own husband. The husband should fulfill his marital duty to his wife, and likewise the wife to her husband."** (1 Corinthians 7:2-3).

The point of this Scripture is to create an *appropriate avenue* of managing and maintaining our sex drives (which by the way, have been given to us by God), in a way that is holy and pleasing to God. We should meet each other's needs within the confines of marriage.

Even though sexual sin has been around since the beginning of mankind, in the Old Testament days I don't think women walked around the Middle East in two piece bathing suits, hot pants or halter tops! Yet, the men of that day were rebuked for their lustful hearts and *"neighing"* *for each other's wife* (Jeremiah 5:8). It's an issue of our wicked hearts, wandering eyes, and perverted minds. This is something we all battle.

A man named Job in the Old Testament, whom God said was "blameless and upright; he feared God and shunned evil" (Job 1:1), had to make a covenant with his eyes *not* to look at the young maidens (Job 31:1). This tells me that even though Job was doing his best to live in a way which was pleasing to God, he still identified with his human side. He dealt with it by acknowledging his proclivity to being weak in this area. He had to make a God-inspired commitment with his heart and eyes. Even though this righteous man was married, he still struggled with lust until he made a choice to combat it and win.

Single men (just like married men) have to rely on the Lord and self control to maintain their sex drives. Most single guys think that married men don't struggle as much as single men in this area. From my studies this simply isn't true. The more sex you have, the more you want. Married men, by and large, expect to be intimate with their wives on a regular basis. When this isn't happening, it can serve to frustrate them more than it would a single man who knows that he isn't going to be sexually active anyway. The difficulty lies in the way single men fuel their sex drives by looking at provocative materials and letting their minds wander continuously on sexual things. If you make a decision as a single man not to inflame yourself with these things, I promise you, God will help you stay strong.

There aren't too many men walking around who can't help noticing a beautiful woman when she walks into the room. It is at this juncture that we men struggle. *Is it wrong to look?* No. However, where we allow our minds to wander in the next 3-4 seconds will determine where our hearts are. Maintaining our integrity *by not looking again* is where the Lord wants our control level to be. She is not your wife, and she is someone else's daughter, including God's. We must come to the godly conclusion of realizing that an attractive woman is a human being made in the image of God. She has been created to be the helpmate of just one man, and it's probably not you.

According to Jesus, lusting with the eyes (the word lusting is "**blepo**" in Greek, and it means to stare with an intense longing and desire), is a sin tantamount (equal) to committing adultery. **The more we practice the control of the eyes through the control of the heart,** the more we will experience victory in the area of simply **noticing** an attractive woman versus **lusting** her.

As married men, we must guard our hearts from being open to the beauty of other women. The women we see and meet are either: 1) married to someone else, or 2) single sisters in Christ whom we are to treat with complete purity (1 Timothy 5:2), or 3) unsaved women in need of salvation. By focusing on the need of a women's heart rather than the beauty of her body, you will be able to see **her spiritual need** rather than

your physical desire. When we see a beautiful woman simply say "**good job God**", and move on. It is an issue of the heart.

When our hearts are pure, then our thoughts are pure. We will then make conscious decisions to not look lustfully in the direction of females. The statement in Titus 1:15 which says, " To the pure, all things are pure", is true indeed. In time, this will become our habit. All of us men need to hold each other accountable to this daily struggle. Find a couple of guys who desire to walk in victory like you do and work on being victorious together. Remember, you will always notice beautiful women but you don't have to be in bondage to lusting them. You can be successful and God will honor your obedience.

CHAPTER THREE

Growing as a Man of God:

FINANCIAL STABILITY & GROWTH

**"Dishonest money dwindles away, but he who gathers
money little by little makes it grow"**
Proverbs 13:11

Did you know that financial problems are the number two cause of divorce? Because we live in a world where "credit" is the order of the day, and that all enticing four letter word "sale" weakens even the most frugal of shoppers, it's no wonder that people live stress-filled lives. In this section we want to walk you through the Biblical principles to financial blessings. At the end of this section you will find a budget sheet to help you on your way to freedom and blessing concerning the stewardship of money.

The world is kept running by the power of economics. There is an old adage which says "The rich get richer and the poor get poorer." This is an axiom that seems to bother a whole lot of people and pleases just a few. The reason that most families struggle financially, is primarily due to the *principles* of handling money. Wealthy people, both Christian and non-Christian alike understand the principles of obtaining financial prosperity. It is important to use the keys that lead to financial blessings, such as good stewardship, hard work, budgeting, and saving, will help put you on the right track and also keep you there. Discipline, which plays a role in every area of our lives, is the cord that ties all these together.

FINDING THE CAUSE AND MAKING A PLAN

If you presently find yourself in a negative financial situation, it is important to understand why. Was it bad luck, poor spending habits, possibly an unforeseen circumstance (a divorce or serious illness), or just a lack of discipline and management? Once you can identify the cause of your financial situation, you can now begin your plans of getting out. The amount of debt you have, your monthly income, monthly expenditures, and the financial commitments you have incurred will determine the duration of your debt period. In addition, how aggressively you want to attack the debt, and your ability to control yourself so as to not further add to it, also play a factor. But without a plan, it's not going to go away on its own.

It has often been said, "It takes money to make money." Although this is true, many millionaires believe if they were to lose everything they could start over and be a millionaire again. The reason they could rebuild is due to their understanding of making and handling money. The Bible gives us the principles we need to manage the money God has enabled us to earn.

There are, of course, significant amounts of money made in the world by dishonest gain, none of which brings lasting happiness or joy. For one thing, the Lord abhors the making of dishonest money. Money made by drug trafficking, swindling, stealing, cheating, not paying taxes, or any other means besides hard work and good business skills will all come back to haunt you - all of it! Proverbs 20:17 says, "Food gained by *fraud* tastes sweet to a man, but he ends up with a mouth full of gravel."

The old sayings of, "Buy low, sell high," "Use your head not your back" and "Work smarter not harder," are just a few good business practices. The principle of Proverbs 14:23 which says, "All hard work brings a profit, but mere talk leads only to poverty" applies to both businessmen and farmers. Many people also make a good living in the labor and construction field, and just about every company would fold if you took away the people who work hard with their muscles.

Farmers and ranchers are some of the hardest workers I've ever met – working from sunup till sundown. Many have prospered from their efforts and hard labor. The Bible gives the secret to prosperity and financial security by using the analogy of the ant; **"Go to the ant you sluggard; consider its ways and be wise!"** (Proverbs 6:6). Wealthy people (businessmen and farmers alike) prosper just like ants do; *they work hard, save, and invest wisely!* The New Testament takes it a step further and says that we are to work for our earthly bosses as though we were working for the Lord (Ephesians 6:7). As one who has owned his own company and now pastors a church of 1,400 people with over 40 paychecks to sign every two weeks, this verse is very valuable to me.

Every boss or company owner wants to feel like they can trust their employees when the boss is not looking.

When an employee has the mindset that they are really working for the Lord Himself and not just the "boss", it has a positive effect on their whole work ethic. We don't have time to go into the great story of Joseph in the book of Genesis to see how he was given promotion after promotion because he worked for his employers as though he were working for God himself.

A Career Change?

There are jobs that don't allow for much growth up the corporate ladder. Some of these jobs unfortunately have a "**financial ceiling**" built in. If you are in a job like this and can barely make ends meet, then you need to see this job as a temporary stepping stone and not a permanent foundation. Sitting down with your spouse (if you are married) or a good friend and talking over your future is a good start at getting ahead.

Let's suppose you are married and have a couple of children at home. You may be saying, "**I work 40 or more hours a week and I barely have enough time for my wife and kids, let alone for myself. I'm tired all the time and feel a little depressed. Besides, I barely make ends meet**." You might ask, "How am I supposed to move on if I'm stuck?" I'm glad you asked. That's the purpose of this section – to help you get ahead financially.

If you currently find yourself in debt, not only do you need to adhere to a budget, but you may also need to come up with a plan where you can get a better return for your investment. *Example:* You work 40 hours a week. You take home $2,000 a month. You are barely getting by and even owe some money. You have no savings going for your children's college fund and you haven't taken a "real" family vacation in years. You may be in debt due to your spending habits, but let's assume for now you just need to make more money.

Your investment at this job is 160+ hours of time and energy each month. The return is merely putting food on the table, clothes for the family, and gas in the tank. Now, this is a good thing, for a man to be able to supply the basic needs of his family. ***Well done!*** If you and your wife are content, and your marriage is working, then maybe this is just where the Lord would want you. But if you are dissatisfied by your present condition because you feel you can get more for your time and energy – let's do something about it.

First, you must sit down with your spouse and share your heart, dreams, feelings, and aspirations and why you have them. (Maybe let her read this section). ***Key note:*** You must be in agreement! If your spouse says she is fine with the present condition and she believes God has you here for a reason, then you need to hear what she is saying and take it to prayer. However, in the near future she shouldn't complain about the finances, since she said this is where you should be. If, however, she agrees that some changes should be made, you need to now formulate a plan.

Let's keep our present scenario, with a husband, wife, and 2 children. I believe the Bible strongly urges mothers, especially of small children, to be keepers at home. Titus 2:3 says, "**Likewise, teach the older women to be reverent in the way they live, not to be slanderers or addicted to much wine, but to teach what is good. Then they can train the younger *women to love their husbands and children, to be self-controlled and pure, to be busy at home*, to be kind, and to be subject to their husbands, so that no one will malign the word of God.**" This is not a command; however, it is highly suggested. Wisdom and experience have taught us the negative effects of mothers not being at home rearing their children.

Unfortunately, in our culture and society, motherhood has been looked down on and some families can't "**keep up with the Joneses**" unless both spouses work. We don't need to go into the statistics of delinquency and divorce to know this is the world's standard and not God's. If we agree that mom will raise the children, which is needed, then man of God, you must make a plan.

There are family situations where it is absolutely necessary that both parents work. In fact, once the children are in school, a job for mom can actually be a positive thing. However, when they are still being weaned at home and they are not in school yet, it seems best for the moms to be at home. But for now, let's look at the husbands income capabilities.

Let's say you've looked into another line of work that gives you a better financial return for your 40 hours. At that job you would be receiving $3,333 per month, or $40,000 per year. It's the same amount of hours, just in a different location, with a different boss signing on the paycheck. It may take you two years on this new job to reach that pay scale, but where will you be two years from now on your current job?

A POSSIBLE PLAN

Let's say you and your spouse agree that for the next 6-12 months (maybe longer) you will give your extra time to the necessary training that will help you achieve your financial goals. You must be honest by agreeing that during this time it will be tough on everybody: you, her, the kids, everybody. You will need to commit to praying together often so the enemy doesn't come in and cause trouble when you are tired or because of the lack of time spent together. Remember, it's only for a short season to reach your long term goals. It will be a sacrifice and a strain, but in the long run you will reap the results. What kind of a job would you enjoy doing? (Be realistic; we are not talking fantasies here, just a realistic job change. If you are 47 years old and you say you want to be a professional football coach and you yourself have never played organized football, you are probably dreaming!).

Where do you get the necessary training? How long will it take? How much will it cost? What is the job market like in this field? These are some of the questions you can begin talking and thinking about. But if you agree that your current job isn't the long term job for you, then plan your career change. **Note to remember**: Do not leave or even slack up on your present job until you are done with the training for the new one and you have a new offer in hand.

First you must determine why you think you need more money, and how you will maintain a higher income budget. Remember, more money doesn't mean more happiness, nor does more money mean that your financial problems will be solved. We usually adjust our spending *up* when we make more money. The principles of handling money are the same if you make $15,000 or $150,000. Usually when people start making more money, they also start spending more. They get a new car, buy some furniture, or join a club, and all of a sudden they find themselves in the same condition as before, if not worse. Once again they think "*If I just made more money.*"

One problem young couples have is thinking that they must have everything their parents had at this time of their life. We must be realistic about our goals and take into consideration the time period our parents grew up in (the cost of living, including the price of a house and car prices) and the time period we live in. Please don't forget the geographic location in which you live. Living in the San Francisco Bay Area in California will cost you much more than living, in let's say, Winnemucca Nevada.

Without planning for the future and saving money strategically and systematically, your dreams may never become a reality. However, if you adhere to God's outline given in His Word and remember that He wants to bless you, He will give you the desires of your heart. Working hard, making an honest living, spending within your means, staying out of credit card debt, and saving little by little, will lead you in the right direction.

Often times singles (especially men) fail to plan financially for marriage and a family. If getting married and having children is your desire, then you must set-up a plan to be able to provide for them. If you are single and just want to have fun and do what you want, spend what you want, come and go as you want, then there is only one person you need to answer to, God! But don't consider marriage until you get it out of your system.

The responsibility for a man to provide for his family's needs (i.e. food, clothes, education, transportation, etc.) can be overwhelming and must be taken seriously. God does want to bless you. Proverbs 18:22 is another verse that does give us comfort that God shall provide for us as husbands. It says **"He who finds a wife finds what is good and receives favor from the Lord."** This includes financial favor as well as other added blessings. However, we must be good stewards over the money God enables us to earn. I want you to know that by following the principles in God's Word you can do it.

What is Debt?

When you begin to buy things that you have not previously saved for or cannot pay off each month, you go into debt. Debt is simply owing money. Some level of debt is acceptable. A mortgage payment on a house, or even a car payment on a necessary car is acceptable, provided it can be afforded by your monthly income. If your budget only allows for a $250 a month car payment, and you get yourself into a $400 a month car payment, you are not using wisdom and you will go into debt.

Let's say you are **not** in debt or at least you are very close to getting out. How do you quickly start saving and getting ahead? There is a book called <u>The Richest Man in Babylon</u> that has a great concept. The basic concept of the book goes like this: there was a man who had become wealthy and he was asked by the King of Babylon to teach the populous how to become rich. His plan was quite ingenious; save at least 10% of what you earn. Live on 90%! Could you live on 90% of your income? Yes, most of us could.

If you made $30,000 a year and you used this formula of saving ten percent, how much will you save in one year? Answer: $3,000. How about in ten years? $30,000. That's not even counting compounding interest! Now this book, <u>The Richest Man in Babylon,</u> wasn't necessarily Biblical in its basis and therefore left out God's added blessings and favors. The key here is to save something each month as a part of your budget. If you can't save 10%, how much can you save?

THE OIL AND WINE CONCEPT

In Proverbs 21:17 it says, "He that loveth **wine** and **oil** shall not be rich" (KJV). Oil and wine speak of the finer things of life; the lavish, extravagant things. Of course extravagant is a relative term. To some, a $50 dinner for two is luxurious living. To others, $50 for dinner is peanuts (pardon the pun!). What this verse is saying is that, if you are spending beyond your means because "you deserve the finer things in life", you will never get ahead financially.

66

You have to determine what you can do without, what is spending beyond your means, and where you can cut some corners. You might feel like saying, "Well, I worked for it, and I deserve a little extravagant living." If this is how you conduct yourself *continuously* then you are not thinking maturely. Yes, especially in America, if you work hard, then you should enjoy the fruit of your labor. However, how often and to what degree? By the way, who said you had to spend a lot to enjoy a good time?

If you didn't complete your education, you keep losing one job after another due to poor work habits or a lack of submission to your superiors; or if you continue to start a job and then quit, you have already had your "good time!" (Some people couldn't finish their education for one reason or another, not just because of 'fun').

Now is the time for planting new seeds, seeds that will produce a profitable harvest. Remember, seed time comes before harvest. What can't be done is spending money that you do not have. If now is seed time, you will have to be patient until harvest time when you will be able to enjoy your "oil and wine."

Who are the Joneses?

Are you trying to keep up with the Joneses? Let me tell you who the Joneses are. They are a group of people in *your mind* whom *you* think are saying, "Be like us; drive a new car, buy a bigger house, wear all designer clothes, eat at posh restaurants." Whoever is doing this is either wealthy or in big time debt! If there actually is someone saying this to you, tell them to hand over the money or the job that will afford this lifestyle and you *will* keep up with the phantom Joneses.

You don't have to spend a lot of money to have a good time. I remember a friend telling me that as he was growing up, his dad was in school to be an optometrist. They didn't have very much money, so for family fun they would go on picnics to the beach, take drives in the country, or play family games. He said those were the most memorable and fun times of his childhood. Whatever you do while you are making financial changes, you must stabilize your spending, set a budget and stick to it, and begin saving and investing. On the next page are some scriptures and principles for financial blessings based on good stewardship.

Again, let me say that finances are simple mathematics; you can't spend more than you take in! If every month you spent $100 more than you made, how much debt will you have in one year? $1200! If you are $300 to $400 above your budget each month you will be $3,600 to $4,800 in debt each year, and that doesn't include interest. Each family must work out their own financial plan. Guys, there is nothing wrong with asking for some help from an Elder in the church or someone who knows finances.
Include your wife in the discussion and that way you won't be one pointing the finger at her.
Take some time with your Bible and read through the scriptures on the next page. I think it will help. If you are married, have your wife go over it with you.

BIBLICAL FINANCIAL PRINCIPLES

(Do yourself a favor and go over these verses prayerfully).

Why God Doesn't Prosper Some People

1) Foolish spending   Proverbs 17:16

2) Luxury isn't for fools   Proverbs 19:10

3) Robbing God   Malachi 3:8-12

How God Will Prosper You

1) Put God First   Matthew 6:33

2) Budget   Proverbs 27:23-24, 21:20

3) Tithes   Proverbs 3:9-10, Malachi
3:8-12, Matthew 22:21

4) Hard Work   Proverbs 10:4-5, 14:23, 20:13, 2
Thessalonians 3:6-10

5) Honest Money   Proverbs 13:11, 11:1

6) Save & Invest   Proverbs 13:22, 19:14

7) Keep a Good Name   Proverbs 22:1 (Don't burn bridges)

8) Help Those in Need   Proverbs 11:24-25, 14:31, 19:17,
Ephesians 4:28

9) Take Care of Family   1 Timothy 5:8, 2 Thessalonians 3:6-
15

Things That Hinder Blessings

1) Dishonest Gain   Proverbs 20:23, 21:6, 22:16, 22:22-23

2) Laziness   Proverbs 20:4, 24:30-34, 18:9

3) Greed   Proverbs 15:27, 23:4-5, 30:7-8, 1 Timothy 6:9-10

4) Foolish Spending   Proverbs 21:17, 25:28, 28:19

5) Unpaid Debts   Psalms 37:21, Proverbs 22:26-27, Romans 13:8

6) Borrowing   Proverbs 22:7, 3:28, 22:26-27

7) Not Paying Taxes   Matthew 22:21, Romans 13:7

8) Forgetting your Provider Philippians 4:19, 2 Corinth 9:6-11

TYPICAL FAMILY BUDGET PLAN

NET MONTHLY INCOME $_____
(What you bring home <u>after</u> Income taxes)

PRIORITIES IN SPENDING (Always Estimate High)

1Tithe (Tenth)
$_____
2Rent or mortgage (include property taxes
                    and house insurance)
                $_____
3Proposed food budget
$_____
  (average monthly spending; high estimate)
4. Health Insurance (medical and dental)
$_____
5. Utilities
        $_____
6. Phone
        $_____
7. Garbage
        $_____
8. Car payment $_____
9. Car insurance $_____
10. Gasoline (average monthly spending) $_____
11. Life insurance $_____
12. Debts (credit cards) $_____
13. School (tuition, daycare) $_____
14. Clothing $_____
15.Miscellaneous toiletries, household,
$_____
    needs, etc.
16Entertainment (dining out, movies, etc.)
$_____
17Investments / savings
$_____
18 Kids activities

19. If self-employed, quarterly taxes
$_____
20.Miscellaneous (car registration, birthday
    party, etc.)
    $_____

TOTAL SPENDING

$_____

(should not exceed Net Monthly Income)

CHAPTER FOUR

Growing as a Man of God:

THE SPIRITUAL SIDE

"The Spirit himself testifies with our spirit that we are God's children"

Romans 8:16

God has given men the awesome responsibility of being leaders in their homes. The enemy (Satan) has tried to strip men of the knowledge and discipline that it requires to accomplish this task in a godly and successful manner. I want to expose the lies, heal the wounds, and bring instruction to all the men who have been struggling in the areas of making godly decisions and being wise leaders. Before you begin reading, would you ask the Lord to give you insight and understanding that will bring you and your family (for those who are married or who have children) to a place of continual harmony? James 3:17-18 says, "But the wisdom that comes from heaven is first of all pure; then peace-loving, considerate, submissive, full of mercy and good fruit, impartial and sincere. Peacemakers who sow in peace raise a harvest of righteousness." Men, as we obey God, we can only be successful!

As the father of three children, I know how difficult the task of being a husband, father, provider, and leader really is. In part, it was because of my many failures that I have been able to write this book for you. I also had the blessing of godly counsel from wise men and their good examples to follow. I have learned that it is *not one thing* that makes you a successful man of God. Rather, it is by applying *all* the principles found in the Word of God that we become victorious.

METHODS AND PRINCIPLES

Most men are either married or want to be married. I have been married for eighteen years with three children, and I can tell you that nowhere is my Christianity tested more than in my relationship with my wife and children. My walk with Christ directly affects my relationship with my family, and the reverse is true also; how I relate to them can affect my walk with Christ. 1 Peter 3:8 says "Finally, all of you, live in harmony with one another; be sympathetic, love as brothers, be compassionate and humble."

My *method* of showing love to my wife may vary depending on the circumstances and situations we may currently be experiencing. For example, if my wife works outside the home, how I show her love and support may be different from how I might show her love if she were a full-time home maker. My method may also change if she were sick or pregnant. If my wife worked outside the home in a full-time job, my methods of showing her love and support might be sharing the cooking and cleaning duties with her, letting her sleep in a little longer on a day off, and things of this nature. If she were a full-time homemaker, I might show my love for her by giving her an hour of "downtime" after I come home from work and have had dinner with the family. During the downtime, I might help the kids with their homework or perform any task that would lighten her load. My method of showing love is dictated by our circumstances.

However, the *principles* of love, sacrifice, kindness, communication, seeking to understand, and forgiveness must never change. It takes prayer and wisdom to be the wise leader of a family. Thank God, He has promised to help us every step of the way!

THE HEAVY RESPONSIBILITY OF BEING A MAN

As a man, you have been called to be a leader. If you are single, you are responsible for yourself and the gifting God has given you (see the parable of the talents – Matthew 25:14-30). However, most men have a desire to be married or remarried. If that describes you, then you have the responsibility of being prepared in all areas for your bride and family.

In as much as you will have to be strong in the areas of finances, self control, and planning ahead, as well as a host of other areas, these are all *secondary* to you being strong *spiritually*. Developing a growing walk with the Lord is what every family needs from the man who is leading them. You have been chosen, ordained, and equipped to do an outstanding job; but you must follow the guidelines set forth in God's Word.

The *spiritual* growth of a man affects the whole man in every

75

area–*emotionally, mentally, physically, and financially.*

How Do I Develop?

The first step in spiritual growth is to *see the need for it.* Since you only live once, and *you are* an awesome individual, you will want to reach the full potential for which God created you. As in every area of your life, you must have a goal, a plan, and the diligence to see it through to **completion**. The goal of this time together is to give some principles of productivity in the spiritual arena that will help you *start* and then *stay* on a path that is both profitable and powerful. You may already be doing some of these things, and that's good. I want to encourage you to continue doing those things that are sound and profitable as well as teach you how to eliminate things that aren't.

2 Peter 1:5 says, "For this very reason, make every effort to add to your faith goodness; and to goodness, knowledge; and to knowledge, self control; and to self control, perseverance; and to perseverance, godliness; and to godliness, brotherly kindness; and to brotherly kindness, love. For if you possess these qualities *in increasing measure, they will keep you from being ineffective and unproductive* in your knowledge of our Lord Jesus Christ" (emphasis mine). What God wants for us is growth in an ever-increasing measure!

As you continue on in your efforts to make changes, you will see yourself developing and so will the people who know you. Of course, not all the changes will be made overnight, but little by little you will know that things in your life are just different.

Don't give up and don't be discouraged. God himself is committed to your

76

progress. Philippians 1:6 says," being confident of this, that he who began a good work in you will carry it on to completion...". It would be good to commit this verse to memory and quote it everyday!

What is the "Spiritual Side" of a Man?

Let's define what we mean by developing the "**spiritual side**" of a man. Spiritual, for our purpose here, is a *relationship* with the God of heaven through His Son the Lord Jesus Christ. Galatians 3:26 says, "**You are all sons of God through faith in Christ Jesus**." When a person comes to God the Father by faith in His son the Lord Jesus Christ, God then gives each person the precious gift of the Holy Spirit (see Acts 2:36-38).

He (the Holy Spirit) is the internal power source from God. The person of the Holy Spirit is our biggest asset in living a quality overcoming life. God, who is in heaven, sent his Son (Jesus) to die and pay for the sins of all humanity and then He (Jesus) went back to heaven and is now sitting at the Father's right hand. This is why He has sent the Holy Spirit to come and live within each believer. The Holy Spirit is our teacher. He empowers us, and comforts us.

The Spirit teaches us the deeper things of God. In 1 Corinthians 2: 9-12 it says,

> "No eye has seen, no ear has heard, no
> mind has conceived what God has
> prepared for those who love him-but God
> has revealed it to us by His Spirit. The

Spirit searches all things, even the deep things of God. For who among men knows the thoughts of a man except the man's spirit within him? In the same way no one knows the thoughts of God except the Spirit of God. We have not received the Spirit of the world but the spirit who is from God, that we may understand what God has freely given us."

The Bible teaches us that we are the temple of the Holy Spirit; this means that God lives in each and every believer. It is from within that He leads and teaches us everything we need to know (Romans 8:9,14).

Also, the Word of God tells us that our confession of **"Jesus as Lord"** and the belief that God raised Him from the dead, has saved us (Romans 10:9-10).

In addition to now having the Holy Spirit, God also has given us His word, the Bible. The Bible guides us in the affairs of life so that we can know the things that God requires of us. The Word and the Holy Spirit teaches us the things that God has chosen to reveal to us about Himself. God is asking us to believe in His love and mercy by faith in Jesus Christ and to stay in communion with Him by prayer as the Holy Spirit teaches us. In addition, as we read His Word regularly and actively obey it, and as we fellowship with other believers consistently, we will grow in an ever-increasing measure.

THREE FOUNDATIONAL CONCEPTS

To see growth from Bible study and prayer, one must have as a foundation at least three things: faith, obedience and a desire to please

God. These things will increase as you walk with Jesus, but you must begin with them. Faith, which God supplies (Ephesians 2:8; Romans 12:3); obedience, knowing that God is the sovereign ruler, our master, and because He has our best interests at heart and can be trusted (John 15:10-11); and a desire to please God, because He first loved us and wants to be involved in every area of our lives (1 John 4:10; 2 Timothy 2:4).

There are those who read the Bible but don't believe what they read. Others read it, believe it, but choose not to obey it. Rather, "they do their own thing", think their own ways, and end up "shipwrecked" both now and for eternity (1 Timothy 1:19). Other people can't seem to stay focused on the things of God, and instead, desire to spend their time doing other things (Matthew 13:22).

If you are going to develop and grow spiritually, you have to believe, obey, and desire the things of God! We will start with the premise that you do desire these three things, and reading this book is going to help you develop them. This is a good start in a great direction!

BEING PART OF THE CHURCH

Being part of a Bible-teaching church is vital to your growth and the growth of your family. The pastor-teacher's job is to teach and expound the Word of God and shepherd the flock. In John MacArthur's commentary on the book of Ephesians he states the following:

> *The pastor-teacher's subsequent work, then,*
> *is to provide the leadership and spiritual resources*
> *to cause believers to be taking on the likeness of*
> *their Lord and Savior through continual obedience*

to His Word and to provide a pattern, or example, of godliness.

This can also be accomplished through other ministries in the church such as men's fellowship, home groups, small group Bible studies, etc. The church should be a safe haven for you and your family. In addition, it should be a place where you can serve God and His people for many years to come.

Being a member of a local church is a design established by the Lord through the Apostles. The church family serves many purposes in helping one another to grow in spiritual maturity, and it will aid you in becoming a man of leadership. You can also bless others by sharing your gifts, talents, and abilities with them. From this, you will see the church that you attend flourish, both spiritually and numerically.

The church setting provides Biblical instruction, accountability, and prayer support. In addition, it provides the opportunity to help meet the needs of others, and it is a place where other men can help carry your burdens. We all need encouragement at times, and being involved in a church family is a wonderful way of receiving that encouragement.

CHOOSING A CHURCH

How can you determine whether a church is a "good" church? There are a few things to look for in choosing a church. Asking God to direct you is a great place to start. Style is obviously going to play a part, but it shouldn't be the primary factor. Is the Word of God being taught in an intelligent and systematic manner? Are you learning and being challenged? Are they preaching against sin? Do you sense the power of the Holy Spirit? What's the vision of the church? Are the people friendly and excited? Is there a men's group? Is the church growing? Where do you fit in? The list can go on and on.

HUNGER FOR GOD'S WORD

If enthusiasm were something I could teach, I would. However, enthusiasm is not taught - it is caught! Having a desire for the Word of God is not only a command, but it is also necessary. 1 Peter 2:2 says, "Like newborn babies, crave pure spiritual milk, so that by it you may grow up in your salvation." God supplies the burning drive to know Him, but it is our responsibility to keep the fire lit! There are so many tantalizing enticements in our lives which stand in opposition to the Word of God; laziness, depression, hedonism (the love of pleasure), amusements (T.V., movies, etc.), greed, sin, workaholism, and many others.

Since most of us live by a schedule (we go to work at a certain time, go to sleep at a certain time, etc.), it is best to schedule times in our day just to commune with God by reading His Word. Christian books and tapes are also good, but it seems nothing can replace the reading of God's *Word* for yourself.

Utilizing sources such as radio, T.V., tapes, videos, and books, can all be of additional value; but they must be carefully screened due to the proliferation of errant doctrine that is now invading the church. If any teaching you encounter doesn't believe in all the basics of Christianity as

81

listed below, please talk with your Pastor. One of the key roles of a Pastor is outlined in Ephesians 4:11-14, which says, "*It was he who gave some to be apostles, some to be prophets, some to be evangelists, and some to be pastors and teachers, to prepare God's people for works of service, so that the body of Christ may be built up until we all reach unity in the faith and in the knowledge of the Son of God and become mature, attaining to the whole measure of the fullness of Christ. That we no longer be infants, tossed back and forth by the waves, and blown here and there by every wind of teaching and by the cunning and craftiness of men in their deceitful scheming.*" My prayer for you is that you develop a hunger for the Word of God which will reward you throughout your whole life (read Psalms 19:7-14).

If *any* of the following tenets (beliefs) of Christianity are not accepted, a person is not genuinely a Christian. The basic tenets are as follows:

1) Jesus existed as God before He was born in a manger.

2) He was born of a virgin and was both fully God and fully man.

3) He lived a perfect sinless life.

4) He physically died on a cross.

5) His blood paid for the sins of everyone in the world.

6) He rose from the dead.

7) He was seen alive by many witnesses.

8) He ascended into heaven.

9) He is coming back one day.

10) You are saved by faith in Christ Jesus through God's grace alone.

Each one of these truths is unequivocally taught in the Bible. We cannot deviate from them lest we begin changing what the Bible and Orthodox Christianity have always taught. You will see upon closer examination that each point is inextricably tied to the other. Untie one, and all Christian teachings unravel.

There are other doctrines or beliefs in Christianity that people can debate or have other views on such as water baptism by sprinkling or complete submersion; is speaking in tongues for today; will the church be raptured into heaven, and if so when? These doctrines and quite a few others are constantly debated. But the foundational truths listed above are the basics which can not be altered. Talk with your pastor about these issues and see what his stance is before joining a church. Your family is depending on you to lead them in the right direction.

Taking a "Spiritual Inventory"

Let's see if we can reestablish a pattern of life that will aid you in all areas of your walk with the Lord. With pencil and paper, take a moment to answer these questions:

1) How long have you been saved?

2) Why did you become a Christian?

3) Define what a "Christian" is.

4) When in your day can you set aside time to read and pray? Be specific.

5) Do you want to know God better?

6) What are some benefits of knowing God better? (See Psalms 103:1-7; list 5 benefits).

7 Attending a Bible-teaching church regularly is a good start to Christian growth. What else will help you develop spiritually?

8) Share your answers with your pastor or a solid Christian whom you can trust.

No Guilt, Only Encouragement

I often ask men if they are praying or reading their Bible. The most common answer I receive is, *"Not as much as I should."* This reply carries a sense of guilt from not having done enough. My response to them is, "How much time *can* you give to Bible reading and prayer?" If they answer, say, 20 minutes a day, I will ask them to begin accomplishing that time goal. If the next time I ask them how they are doing in these two areas and they tell me, "Not as much as I should," then I know that they are struggling to reach their 20 minute goal.

Each of us must determine, according to our own schedule, how much time we can honestly give to prayer and Bible reading and then make it a goal. This will require discipline, and remember, we are not looking for a quota, nor is this a law; we are trying to develop a relationship with our God. In fact, there may be some weeks when your schedule is more "bogged down" than other weeks and you may not get to spend as much time with the Lord as you want. But don't let that be your normal pattern. Here are some ideas and methods for Bible reading and prayer that may prove helpful.

A) Bible study

1) The systematic approach. Read one chapter after another, and one book after another. For example, read Matthew 1 through the end at chapter 28; then Mark 1-16, etc. Or, read one Gospel, then one epistle. Another way is to start in Genesis and read through the Old Testament. The purpose of this is to see the big picture of what each author is saying. This approach also teaches you discipline.

2) The topical method. This is where you study one specific topic, such as love, money, sin, or parenting. Search for the related *passages* and *stories* in the Bible that pertain to one subject. This is a good approach when you are weak in a certain area, or just need knowledge about a specific issue. The reason I say **"passages"** and **"stories"** is because a passage often gives you the direction, command or concept. For example, Ephesians 6:4 says "Fathers, do not exasperate your children; instead bring them up in the training and instruction of the Lord." This is a command to follow and obey. The difficulty is that this verse doesn't give a detailed explanation of how to do this. I must read Old Testament stories or use the outline of Paul in writing to Timothy or Titus as a father to a son to glean some insights on the "how-to's" of being a dad. This type of study is fun and the insights are almost endless.

3) The biographical method. This method can be the funnest of all. Pick a Bible character, such as David, Paul, or Hannah and study their lives. It will amaze you how much we are all alike. The reason these are so enjoyable is because we humans all have the same problems in general; even the famous people of the Bible.

My suggestion would be to start with the systematic approach in the New Testament. Once you get going, you will then want to read the Old Testament accounts found in the first 39 books of the Bible. The stories are enjoyable and you will see a mirror of yourself as you read through its pages. Try to read slowly enough to really understand. And don't worry about retaining everything you read. The Holy Spirit will remind you of what you need to remember. This is a life long race, not a short sprint to the finish line.

I will admit, for young Christians, some passages like the first few chapters of Leviticus, for example, may seem boring. At first, it might not mean much; but later you will see the need for it. Also, some of the writing from the prophets can be difficult for young believers to understand. This is why I suggest reading the New Testament first.

God has chosen to reveal Himself to us in His word. You can only know Him and His ways by reading the Word and listening to people teaching the Word. *Probably the most difficult part of Bible study is taking the time to do it.* For most of us, our schedules control us rather than us controlling them. We fail to realize just how scheduled our lives really are. We have to be at work at set times, go to bed at set times, and watch our favorite T.V. shows at set times. *Unless we plan when we will read the Bible, or pray, or go to church, for that matter, we may seldom get around to it.* Once we see the value of Bible reading we can better understand the need for making and taking the time to read the Word. Look at it this way: it is *God's blueprint* for building our lives.

Whenever my wife and I have purchased something that must be put together by the consumer (us), my wife is much better at it than I am. It's not that she is necessarily anymore "handy" than I am or "light years" brighter. It's simply because she stops to read the instructions! I want to figure it out on my own. I mean who has time to sit and read a bunch of "fine print"? Invariably, when I'm done, if I ever get done, I have parts left over. I reason, "They just provided extra parts in case some of us 'slower' people lose them."

God's Word is our instruction booklet for life. It directs us in each area from handling money to parenting, from communication to gardening. You name it, when it comes to managing our lives for success, it is written!

B) Prayer

Prayer, which is equally as powerful and important as Bible reading, has other distinct benefits. There are at least 10 different ways of praying:

1) Praise: for what He has done and who He is

2) Confession: for any and all sin

3) Thanksgiving: for salvation, the Holy Spirit, blessings, what He has done, etc.

4) Petition: for things you need or desire

5) Intercession: praying for other people & situations

6) Meditation: for thinking on God, His Word and life

7) Communion: for simply talking to God and spending time

with Him

8) Worship: for who He is

9) Praying the Word: for applying God's promises to our situation, or ourselves, or for combating the devil.

10) Praying in other tongues: for speaking to God in an unknown language by the Spirit.

Just like Bible study, prayer takes a commitment of time and effort. Anything that we do which causes us to be more effective in our Christian walk will be met with opposition from our adversary, the devil. He will do whatever he can to stop you from a concentrated time of communion with God. If he can't get you to sin, he'll keep you busy! It seems like the phone always rings, the kids have an argument, someone's at the door, or our minds want to drift on to things that are insignificant. Add to that our lack of discipline to do what we know we ought to do, and we can quickly become defeated in our pursuit of drawing close to God.

But, thank God, He has given us His Spirit which enables us to be self-controlled so that we can accomplish those things which are profitable for us.

A PRAYER CLOSET

Finding a "prayer closet" and a set time of prayer is vital to your growth as a Christian and also to you being a leader in your home. A prayer closet can be anyplace where you can be alone with the Lord (preferably without interruption) so that you can both talk with the Lord and listen to Him.

When I was first saved, I lived at my parent's home and I was not married yet. For one hour each night I would take my dog for a walk around the neighborhood. That became my prayer closet. In more recent years the church sanctuary became my quiet place of prayer. Once you take the time and find a place for prayer, you will covet these times and become irritated when they are interrupted or neglected. Become the most faithful and devoted person of prayer that you know. Why? It will change your life!

A PRAYER PARTNER

The devil wants us to underestimate the power of prayer. James 5:16 says, "Therefore confess your sins to each other and pray for each other so that you may be healed. The prayer of a righteous man is powerful and effective." Like anything else in life, the more you do something the better you become at it. Sometimes finding a prayer partner can be a great aid in building a prayer life. The two of you can agree on things to pray for. You can keep each other accountable and encourage one another along the way. You can also share praise reports as God continually answers your prayers and acts on your behalf. Don't let prayer be something you do only when you are in need or in trouble. Let it be a daily relationship with your Heavenly Father.

Some people pray in their car on the way to and from work. Although this may seem to be the only time available in which to pray, it is not the best approach because you still have to concentrate on driving! It is important to have a time when your undivided attention is given to God for prayer. However, praying in your car is better than not praying, and God is definitely listening. Suggestion: If you pray while driving, don't pray with your eyes closed! Prayer: Don't live life without it!

Tips for Married Men

If you are married, your wife most likely would like you to initiate a family Bible reading and prayer time. As the leader of your family, when you turn off the TV and pray with your family, and maybe even have communion with them, it brings such a sense of security, comfort, and peace. In the long run this will pay big dividends. Some couples find it hard to pray together. They feel prayer is more of a private matter. You may want to begin by agreeing on things to pray about. Write down an outline for your family goals. You may want to include things like seeing all of the children saved, family finances, or whatever issues may come up at any given time.

According to statistics, one out of every two marriages ends in divorce. Another study showed that couples who pray together have a divorce rate of 1 in 1,152! I would greatly encourage couples to pray together, even if at first it is only praying in agreement about the same things. You will begin to see a sense of peace come over your home. If your wife resists at first, don't be discouraged, pray for her and forgive her every day.

In Conclusion

As your prayer and Bible study habits develop and become consistent, you will begin to see a positive impact on your life. There is one catch, however: *obedience!* As you read God's Word, or the Holy Spirit impresses something on your heart in prayer, obedience is what turns it into a reality and a blessing for you. Jesus said, "If you love Me, you will obey what I command" (John 14:15).

As a loving father, you would never tell or ask your children to do something that would be harmful to them. You always have their best interest in mind. We have a Father who really does know best. He knows the beginning from the end, and everything in between. Colossians 2:3 tells us that "...Christ, in whom are hidden all the treasures of wisdom and knowledge." James 1:5 says that "If any of you lacks wisdom, He should ask God." You and I both know that we lack wisdom in so many different areas. What a privilege to know that God says that we can come to Him for anything we need. James 4:2 says, "You do not have, because you do not ask God." God desperately desires to answer our prayers! Let's take advantage of our privilege to ask God for the things we need. Remember, He places the desires in our hearts and then He grants those desires (see Psalms 37:4).

If you are not currently in a good Bible teaching church, begin asking God to lead you to one, preferably close to home. Get yourself involved in a men's group at church where discipleship is encouraged.

Rearrange your schedule in a realistic manner whereby you have quality time in prayer and the Word. Once you determine how much time that is, do your best to commit to it. Make it a goal to join with your wife in spiritual things. As you align yourself spiritually, you are on your way to becoming the man that God has created you to be. There are many other facets to the spiritual growth side of our lives; things like integrity, keeping promises, being a godly example to the family, living with your wife in an understanding way, etc. For now, we have laid the foundation.

CHAPTER FIVE

Growing as a Man of God:

THE EMOTIONAL SIDE

"But you, keep your head in all situations..."
2 Timothy 4:5

Emotions, what are they? Where do they come from? How do we control them? We are going to unfold the truth and power of these God-given feelings which can be either a source of healing and strength, or they can be destructive to the point of hurting yourself or someone else.

Like everything else God gives us for our good, emotions must be managed and controlled. Emotions are powerful, and they often lead us, rather than our leading them. A wild stallion is a powerful animal and very useful to us when it has been brought under control and trained to do what we want it to do. However, a stallion that is unbridled or untrained can be very dangerous. Emotions, because of their ability to control *while being out of control,* can also be very dangerous.

Emotions were given to us as a part of our human make-up. *The emotion of anger isn't the problem,* it's how we manage it that determines our success or failure. How we manage anger or any other emotion that causes us problems is directly related to how we think and the choices we make. Let's take a closer look at these powerful feelings called emotions.

Just What are Emotions?

Webster defines emotion as, "strong feeling; excitement; a state of consciousness having to do with the arousal of feelings, distinguished from other mental states...any of various complex reactions with both mental and physical manifestations..." We tend to use words like compassion, sympathy, and empathy, to describe how we feel. More commonly we use words like, sad, happy, depressed, joyful, or angry, to describe our emotions. Could you imagine what life would be like without emotions? Now some of you might say, "it would be great not to have anger, or to ever be depressed or sad," but could you also imagine what it would be like to not experience joy or happiness, or to feel compassion? As humans, we are made up of all these emotions and more, and God knew just what he was doing.

These "feelings" are a result of how we think or the way we process the information that passes through the brain. *Think about that!* My brain processes information that determines how I will feel. How do you feel about that? Let me explain. When I hear that my team has just scored a touchdown, my brain takes this information and instantly processes it. My brain already knows what it wants to hear if things were to go my way, and this causes a feeling of joy or happiness. My body may or may not react, depending on the control I use to govern it. This is why one person may jump up and spill the popcorn on the people in front of them while screaming at the top of their lungs, whereas another person may sit in a very stoic manner and only smile. We are constantly training ourselves to respond to life's events. There are times when we will have a heightened sense of excitement or feel discouraged more than usual. However, what we want to find is a balance.

FINDING A BALANCE

I once knew a guy who one day could be extremely happy and the next day extremely sad. When I brought this to his attention, he said, "I guess I'm just an extreme person." I said, "How about being extremely balanced?" If we can learn to control how things affect us by properly thinking through our attitudes and actions, life won't be such an "emotional roller coaster." How do I learn to control my feelings when things aren't going the way I would like?

First, I must realize that not everything is going to go my way. Unmet expectations can be the biggest culprit in our feelings of anger or frustration. Proverbs 13:12 admonishes us that "hope deferred makes the heart sick..." In other words, if something that I have been waiting for and expecting doesn't happen when I need it or want it to, it can bother me way down on the inside. What usually angers or frustrates us are things not going the way we would like or want them to. Maybe we should write a new song entitled, "I'd Like It My Way."

Here's a question for us to answer: "Is getting upset or bummed-out going to change the circumstances?" Probably not. Then I must make a choice to not respond *how I feel like responding.* Rather, I must control how I will respond. In its simplest form, it is a matter of choice. *With the strength of the Holy Spirit, I must choose to not give in to "feelings" as*

95

my controller. You might say, "Well, that seems easy to say, but is it really possible when I have always responded in anger or other inappropriate ways?" I'm glad that you asked. Remember, we respond based on how we think and the habits we have formed. Controlling anger comes from learning how to think properly, being led by the Spirit, and learning new habits of response. Let me explain how our anger problems originated.

FOUR STEPS TO UNDERSTANDING ANGER

Step 1. We were born angry.

We must realize that unrighteous anger is rooted in our sin nature. We inherited our "anger problem" from Adam after the Fall of Man in the garden. Uncontrolled anger is a work of the flesh, our fallen nature. Now, you might ask, "If it's a part of my humanity, how will I ever get rid of it?" Hang on, and I'll show you. When we are walking "in the flesh", we can produce all kinds of attitudes that are not only sinful but can also be very destructive.

The first human with a bellybutton, Cain (Adam and Eve were created not born), was the first to inherit his dad's (Adam's) sin nature. Within that new nature were things like anger and jealousy. Because of his jealousy towards his brother Abel, Cain was told by God, "...sin is crouching at your door; it desires to have you, but you must master it" (see Genesis 4:1-7). Anger that was out of control, fueled by jealousy, actually changed the course of his life. God was warning him in advance, "If you don't control yourself, your anger will control you" (paraphrased).

Jealousy, especially in relationships, can lead to abnormal behavior. The prisons are full of people where a third party came between lovers and murder became the end result. Proverbs 27:4 says, "Anger is cruel and fury overwhelming, but who can stand before jealousy?" Being angry over something that is wrong or unfair in and of itself is not sin; it's how far you take it or it takes you that becomes the problem.

What we inherited from Adam in the garden is in direct opposition to the new and heavenly nature given to us by God. Self-control is a fruit of the Spirit while anger that is sinful is from the flesh nature. When anger is not controlled it will always lead to inappropriate and possibly destructive behavior.

Step 2. Anger is fueled by people offending us or letting us down.

All of us have unmet expectations, and all of us have been hurt by things that people have done to us. Hurt causes feelings of anger that will probably be shown by improper outward manifestations. We think that people shouldn't hurt us or let us down. After all, "We wouldn't do that to other people; and if we ever did, we sure didn't mean to, so why are they getting so upset?" However, since we do not live in a perfect world, people will always hurt us or let us down. We must learn to change our response. Once we analyze why we feel angry, which is done by taking in all the facts concerning any particular situation, we may find it is nothing more than our pride getting hurt because we did not get our own way. Let me say at this point, however, that there is an anger, a righteous anger, which is not a sin.

Ephesians 4:26 says, "In your anger do not sin." Paul is saying that we have been given emotions by God for which we are to be responsible. *The emotion of anger in and of itself is not a sin.* It leads us into sin when we respond out of proportion to the offense which has been committed, that is, if there indeed has been an offense committed. There are times when anger *is* the proper response, and your voice may need to be raised, or you may react in a way that isn't part of your normal behavior.

A scriptural case in point is when Jesus, **twice**, rebuked the money-changers and sellers in the temple courts (most Bible commentators see the account in John 2:13-17 in the first year of Jesus' ministry and the one recorded in Matthew 21:12-13, Mark 11:15-17, and Luke 19:45-46 in the third year of his ministry. This author agrees with that view). Jesus was infuriated at the lack of reverence being displayed by the so-called religious leaders. They were selling sacrifices that the people needed to offer at exorbitant prices. Still others who were able to bring their own sacrifices were told that the sacrifices they were bringing were not acceptable to God. They were then forced to buy the temple sacrifices at inflated prices. When Jesus saw their hypocrisy and greed, he responded with righteous indignation. Some might say, however, that Jesus wasn't acting very "**Christlike**" or, was He?

Righteous indignation, which is anger that acts against sinful or ungodly situations, responds according to the crime committed. Jesus was completely justified to act this way against the hypocrisy of the religious leaders who were supposed to be the examples for the people. James 3:1 says, "Not many of you should presume to be teachers, my brothers, because you know that we who teach will be judged more strictly." Jesus' words "Get these out of here! How dare you turn my Father's house into a market!", were justified given the context. The religious rulers were not teaching truth and in turn were ripping off the people financially and all this was being done at God's Temple! Jesus had every right to respond this way.

Yet, even in righteous anger, self-control must be used, or unnecessary words or actions will be displayed. This is why King David said to the Lord, "Oh Lord, do not rebuke me in your anger or discipline me in your wrath." (Psalm 6:1, Psalm 38:1). David knew that if God punished him in His anger, He might "spank" too hard. This is something that every parent should listen to. If God as our Heavenly Father could dole out "too much" punishment when angry, then how much more should we earthly parents make sure that we are calm before we chastise. There are isolated times when righteous anger is necessary. However, for most of us, outbursts of anger are far too frequent and far to intense than the situation usually calls for. So, understanding that step two, being offended or let down, becomes fuel for step one gives me a little more insight as to the genesis of anger. Since I'm born with anger, an offense gives my sin nature a chance to express itself.

Step 3. We have been around people with "anger problems".

We develop patterns of anger by being associated with people who have a difficult time controlling their anger. The Bible says, "Do not make friends with a hot-tempered man, do not associate with one easily angered, or you may learn his ways and get yourself ensnared" (Proverbs 22:24-25).

You watch people who raise their voice or say whatever they "feel" like saying, so you raise yours, and pretty soon you have developed a pattern of anger. Oftentimes it was a dad or mom who displayed this kind of behavior and you picked it up yourself. Once anger is in control of your life as a habit, it is like putting your feet in fast drying glue. It is not easy to get out, and some people never do! Can you think of a person in your life who has modeled uncontrolled anger to you? Even though you would have never engaged a dad or mom in a yelling match (even though many young people do), by not engaging them means you had to remain passive. This caused you to repress your feelings and as you got older, these pent up feelings began to be expressed. Now you "let loose" whenever you feel the need. Think back for a moment: How long have you been displaying inappropriate anger and from whom did you learn it?

Step 4. We have developed habits of anger.

Anger is a part of our makeup. People let us down or offend us, and because we have been around people who have modeled a lack of control concerning their emotions, *we* have developed patterns and habits of inappropriate behavior concerning the handling of *our* emotions. This is why we see so many people who just can't seem to control their anger. When they get angry, they act out of "developed habits" that are not controlled. Anger, even when it is justified, does not give us a license to behave inappropriately.

Again, let me say, *righteous anger* produces behavior that is necessary and needed, yet controlled. When someone else is in the wrong, that does not give us the right to react in ways which are not under control.

It is never the right thing to cuss, call people names simply to hurt them, or let emotions fly which are out of proportion to the offense. This is anger that is controlling us rather then us controlling the emotion.

Also there are times when *we have been in the wrong* or it was our fault, and out of our frustration we made someone else pay the tab (usually it is the people closest to us, i.e. spouse, kids, family, etc.). We are really bothered with ourselves, but we shift the object of our anger (ourselves) to someone who had nothing to do with the situation. All of a sudden we yell at them, tell them off, physically threaten them or worse. We must learn new ways of dealing with the circumstances of life. It is difficult at first because we are learning and developing new habits, but it is not impossible.

The Solution

So how do we walk in continual victory over this "all consuming fire" that constantly wants to burn? Like with any fire, you have to take away its fuel! When we are Holy Spirit-controlled, and we understand what it takes to control anger, we can then begin changing negative patterns. We must realize that anger isn't conquered *"once and for all."* It is sometimes a daily conquering. **PLEASE REMEMBER THIS!** You continually conquer anger each time it tries to take over. You *can* come to a place where it would take something absolutely monumental to cause you to lose your cool. But controlling anger is a daily job.

However, even when you have reached that level of control, you must guard and protect the ground that you have gained or you can slip right back into the uncontrolled patterns. Once I realize that I will always have to face the potential of my anger "rearing its ugly head," I must remain watchful concerning my **actions and reactions**. As already stated, by being Holy Spirit led and having understanding, I can begin to conquer this. The first few times it may seem impossible, but you <u>can</u> do it. Don't let anyone tell you that you can't, even yourself!

Now that we have a better understanding of where anger originated from, how it began to grow, people who helped teach me negative patterns of anger management, and that over the years I have developed my own negative patterns, I will show you how to reverse this curse.

4 Steps In – 4 Steps Out

Step 1. Brand new.

After realizing that we are born with anger as a part of our human make-up, I must be ***born again*** spiritually to override my sin nature. By this I mean accepting Jesus Christ as my personal savior, whereby God gives me His Spirit and changes my nature. This is what I mean by being born-again. God gives us a new spiritual nature, His! When the Holy Spirit comes to live in us, our own human spirit becomes alive to God. Romans 8:10 says, "But if Christ is in you, your body is dead because of sin, yet your spirit is alive because of righteousness." What a great exchange, our old nature for His new one!

But the fruit of the Spirit is love, joy, peace, patience, kindness,

102

goodness, faithfulness, gentleness, and self control (Galatians 5:22). Once I understand that I'm born again and "uncontrolled sinful anger" is *not* a part of my new nature, I don't have to let anger or any other sin control me (see Romans chapters. 6-7).

In Ephesians 5:18, Paul said, "Do not get drunk on wine, which leads to debauchery. Instead, be filled with the Spirit." As we allow ourselves to be filled and thus controlled by the Holy Spirit, we have a great head start on not allowing our sin nature to steer our emotional ship. Being filled with the Spirit is done by fellowshipping with the Lord through prayer, worship, meditation, praise, and study of the word. Obedience is the final key to success in any area of our Christian walk. **Step one is being born again with God's new spiritual nature.**

Step 2. Proper evaluation.

Once I realize that people are sinful and sometimes ignorant, that they will sometimes hurt me maliciously or by accident, and that they *will not* meet my expectations, I can be more realistic in my expectations. By having realistic expectations, I am not as disappointed, and therefore my emotional response is more reasonable. Sometimes my expectations are unreasonable and unrealistic towards people and sometimes I don't make my expectations known. By not thinking through these issues and more, I set myself up to be let down. However, even if I am let down, how will I respond? *Step two then is a two-step process!*

A) Forgiveness.

Remember, if I'm born with anger as a part of my nature and being Born Again is what offsets this, and if offenses fuel my anger problem, then removing the offenses through forgiveness is the beginning of part two. I must choose to *forgive* the party who has offended me. As a Christian, this is not an option. It is not only a step of obedience, it is what sets me free from the offense which is making me so angry. If what someone did to me is causing me to become angry, my willingness to remove the offense through talking and forgiveness now allows me to think and act as though no offense had ever taken place.

What are my options if I don't forgive? I can get angry every time I see this person or think about what he/she has done to me. I can add this offense to all the other offenses I haven't forgiven, but, by doing this, I will be in a perpetual state of anger. By not forgiving people (including forgiving ourselves), I am empowering them to control my life, even when they are not around. They probably aren't even aware that I'm feeling so angry. Do I really want people to control me like this? According to God's Word, I choose to forgive each and every offense against me. This removes the fuel that usually keeps our anger blazing. This will also include people who have hurt us or let us down from years past.

This anger, when not scripturally dealt with, has a negative effect far beyond simply not handling yourself properly. Anger turned inward is a root cause of depression. Depression can also be caused by viewing ourselves improperly, chemical imbalances, or things which we valued highly but didn't turn out the way we wanted. All too often it is caused by not forgiving someone, including ourselves, and letting it fester inside of us. Release this pent up anger by way of forgiveness and walk in the joy of the Lord! (I will talk more about depression in a moment).

B) A new perspective.

The second part of step two is to **think** and **talk** your way to calmness. I must not empower people to let me down to the point of controlling my emotions. I can accomplish this by properly assessing each situation and realizing that people are just people. We humans are incapable of perfection; there is no way that we/they will always do what we want or think. Therefore I must have a fair and reasonable expectation level of what I think others will do or should do in certain situations. Here's an example: Have you ever been "cut off" on the freeway? What usually happens when you get cut off? You get this sudden rush of heat up through your neck, face, and head. You think, "How could that jerk do that?" You're right, in a perfect world, it shouldn't happen. But, we don't live in a perfect world; we live in a sin-filled world. I'm not saying that such selfish maneuvering on his part shouldn't cause you some feelings, but how far do you take it? Do you cuss him out, crash him, track him down and kill him? Why empower this person to control you like that? Now you might say, "He's not controlling me." Really? Then who is? You're not!

Is it possible that this guy's wife is sick and dying in the hospital, and the reason he is driving sporadically is due to the fact that he is trying to get there before she dies? Let me ask another question. What was your reason or excuse the last time you cut someone off? Did you get upset when the other person was bothered with your inconsiderate driving? Isn't it amazing? We get bothered when others "cut us off," *and we get bothered when they get bothered because we cut them off!* *(Think about that).*

Ephesians 4:26 says, "**Be ye angry, and sin not...**"(KJV) Controlling our anger is done by thinking properly and being Spirit-controlled. *Stop and think.* *How often is our anger level out of proportion to the offense that has been committed? Whether it's to our spouse, kids, parents, or co-workers, we are simply over-reacting or improperly reacting to each offense.* So often we use an axe to kill the fly on our neighbor's forehead!

Let's talk about that time you or I cut someone else off on the freeway. Sometimes we had no good reason other than we were just acting like a jerk. Do you remember what we wanted after we cut them off? For them to forgive us! **We want people to forgive us quickly when we make a mistake or do something mean or stupid.** If they don't, we get offended and angry because they won't forgive us. Now we hold onto this *new* offense of them not being willing to forgive us for our offense *(read that again)*. A sad "merry-go-down" in deed. We must be willing to get off this ride. Matthew 5:7 says, "Blessed are the merciful, for they will be shown mercy."

Step 3. Finding a person who is self-controlled as the new model for me to copy.

I must see a new vision in my mind of how I want to act and respond. If, let's say, my dad was the person who acted out his anger in

106

improper ways, then I grew up learning to be just like him. I need to keep telling myself that I don't want to be like that. However, the picture I then have in my mind is one of whom *I'm not trying to be like*. But then, whom do I want to be like? Ponder that for a moment. What picture do I have in my mind of the person I want to be like? Is there a person in your life who seems to control themselves fairly well? Spend a little time with this person and ask him/her to help you. By imitating this person, you will establish new habits and patterns. Finding people who are self-controlled is a major key to victory.

As stated earlier, Galatians 5 contrasts *the works of our sin nature* (anger being one of them) *and the fruit of the Spirit* (of which one is self control). See a picture of yourself being full of love, joy, peace, patience, kindness, goodness, faithfulness, gentleness, and self-control. Seeing what you want is a key to success. I don't want to look at a picture of what I do **not** want to be. I must visualize the proper responses and reactions if I want to be victorious.

If I want to improve my looks, **not** trying to look like Frankenstein is **not what I want to focus on**. I'm going to find someone I do want to look like and focus on their qualities. Set a goal for yourself of the kind of person you want to be and then practice it everyday of your life. And let me add that, not only do I want to find a new example to be like, I want to be the example of the kind of person others can be like. It comes down to thinking right.

Philippians 4:8-9 gives us an outline of what we are to think about concerning ourselves and situations in our lives. It instructs us to think on things that are true, noble, lovely, admirable, excellent, or praiseworthy.

107

Why we become increasingly angry is due to what we are allowing our minds to focus on. *The ability to take and keep control of how we feel and act, is directly related to how we think.* My new goal is to be a person others can copy.

Step Four: I must develop new patterns and habits in my life.

I must think through situations that make me angry and make a choice to be led by the Holy Spirit instead of "giving in to the flesh." How many times have you lost your cool and felt like an idiot afterwards? How did you allow yourself to get to that point, or worse yet, why do you continue to let yourself get to that point? Each day that you practice self-control, you become better at it. You are forming new habits of proper responses to replace or exchange the old ones of simply losing your cool.

How many times have you said things in anger unnecessarily? You probably would have saved an argument had you controlled your tongue and chose words that were not emotionally driven. You really can learn new ways of reacting, but you must begin practicing today. It is not going to get better if you don't start now. Begin by saying a prayer of repentance for having allowed anger to dominate your life in many instances. Picture yourself staying calm and using logic instead of intimidation, abusive words, and aggressive body language. Ask the Holy Spirit to fill you and to empower you to be more self-controlled and think about situations ahead of time.

Habits are things we simply do on a regular basis as a way of life. If you are losing your cool regularly, it is because after continued improper responses these responses became your pattern and habit. So now we are practicing new patterns and habits. Listen, you can do it; but you must begin trying now. Make a commitment to yourself that the next time you face a situation in which you would normally "let-er-blow", you will speak calmly and handle the situation like a man under control.

There are a couple of ways to learn from the Scriptures. One way is to **study** and **obey** Scriptures like Philippians 4:8-9, or Galatians 5:22-23. Another way is to read related stories and learn from their failures or successes. For example, in the story of David coming to bring bread and roasted grain to his brothers, his oldest brother became angry with him and spoke very unkindly to David. He began to insult him and judge his motives while "shooting down" his character (1 Samuel 17:28-29). So often anger causes us to "disengage" our brains and we speak words that are cutting and damaging. In another story concerning King Saul, he was unequivocally trying to get rid of David. Jonathan, his son, didn't want to believe it so he tested his dad by coming up with a plan. When Saul realized that Jonathan was helping David out, in his anger, he hurled his spear at Jonathan, trying to kill him (1 Samuel 20:33).

You can get so angry at a person that you become blinded to what you are doing at that moment. It isn't until the damage has been done or your anger has subsided that you realize the absurdity of your actions. By reading these stories we often see a mirror of ourselves and this can help us think differently concerning how we will now act.

A classic case is found in Genesis 34. In this story, Dinah, the only daughter of Jacob, was molested by a man who couldn't control his sex drive. When Dinah's brothers Simeon and Levi heard about it, they were furious. Later, at an opportune time, Simeon and Levi overreacted in their anger and the punishment they delivered in return was a greater sin than the one committed against their sister.

Later in Genesis 49:5-7, when their father Jacob was ready to die and it was time to bless his kids, all he could say to Simeon and Levi was "…their swords are weapons of violence. Let me not enter their council, let me not join their assembly, for they have killed men in their anger and hamstrung oxen as they pleased. Cursed be their anger, so fierce, and their fury, so cruel! I will scatter them in Jacob and disperse them in Israel."

There are also many accounts of people who *have* controlled themselves even when they may have had a *right* to respond in a vindictive manner. When looking at the opposite side of this encounter between Saul and David, you find David twice in a position to harm Saul for chasing him without a cause. But each time David restrained his emotions and thought properly. This enabled him to act with control. *When someone has committed a wrong, that does not give you the right to retaliate.* "Do not take revenge, my friends, but leave room for God's wrath, for it is written: 'It is mine to avenge; I will repay,' says the Lord." (Romans 12:19). Stop, think, and do the right thing!

LIKELY SITUATIONS

Let's say a housewife has had a tough day with the kids and her husband is due home any moment. What she needs is understanding and a short break. Without ever saying a word, her *need* has now become an expectation in *her* mind. Her husband walks in the door, having had a difficult day himself and is in *need* of a hug and a cool soda-pop. *His* need, in his mind, is now an expectation. He walks in and and looks to her to make the first move, while at the same time she is looking to him to make the first move.

He finally speaks up with a touch of frustration in his voice and says, "Sure would be nice to get a little respect around here." This one statement sends hot flashes up her neck and face and she retorts with, "Yeah, it would be nice to get a break from serving everybody all the time." His anger increases and he makes an even more insensitive comment back, and now she is ready "to put on the boxing gloves."

Three things need to take place to change this outcome from getting really ugly. First, they must stop and calm down. *Someone has to take control, by getting in control.* The second thing is to try and understand the other person. What was it that he/she was looking for? And lastly, they must both realize that they each had unspoken expectations that were left unmet. This caused hurt feelings which resulted in anger that took control of their words and actions.

There will always be things that we can become angry about. We must determine what is worth getting upset over, and then, to what degree. We must also determine what is a minor offense that doesn't need a response at all and that required some discussion. In 2 Timothy 2:24 Paul says, **"And the Lord's servant must not quarrel..."** Keeping a calm attitude in every situation, as much as possible, is done by thinking properly. When there is something to get upset over, staying controlled enough to not get carried into sin is accomplished by quickly determining

111

just how upset am I going to allow myself to get regarding this issue. Believe it or not, you can begin to live out positive patterns of self-control. This is the will of God.

LOSING CONTROL

Losing control, or more appropriately, when our emotions are now controlling us, becomes evident anytime we are acting in a manner in which we should be acting differently. You know you're not in control when you rationalize it by saying, "I'm sorry, I just can't help it." This is often demonstrated in forms such as loud talking, cussing, saying mean or spiteful things, being physical (punching, kicking, throwing things), giving the other person "the silent treatment," complete withdrawal, outbursts of rage, threats, and things like these.

Especially in men, anger is often associated with pain. Not necessarily physical pain, although this is included. I am referring to feelings of being rejected, or unfair treatment, jealousy, or the challenging or insulting of the male ego. Sometimes we men allow ourselves to get emotionally "charged up" when statements are made that nullify the **efforts we have put out to help or bless others.** I'm not saying it's acceptable; it's not, but men have a difficult time restraining their feelings when this happens.

Our values (or what we deem important) will determine how we respond in a given situation. Each of us has to examine which are the likely scenarios that normally "set us off." Unfortunately, in most cases, because anger is such a habit, it really doesn't matter what might take place. If it is something we don't like we are probably going to respond with anger. However, if we can determine when we may get bothered and why, we can then set a strategic plan of "counter attack" by preparing ourselves in advance to respond differently.

Let me add an additional note here; being intoxicated by foreign substances like **drugs or alcohol** greatly increases your *inability* to respond in a proper manner and also continues the pattern of anger in your life.

Fatigue is another factor that can affect our attitudes and behavior. Think about this: when are babies most likely to cry or throw fits? Usually when they are tired, hungry, wet, or aren't feeling well. They also throw fits when they don't get their way! Scary, but it sounds like adults too, doesn't it? When we are aware of the "buttons" that "set us off," we can better prepare to conquer them. This is of paramount importance.

Let's say that you lose your cool when one of your children forgets something or doesn't respond to your requests quickly enough. You must now determine if you are being unreasonable. This again has to do with the unmet expectations which we spoke about earlier. If the child's behavior is unacceptable, you must now decide what is the appropriate response to the situation. Too often we hand out a **"life sentence for jaywalking!"** Is there a reason we can't say the same words calmly? Consider the last time you lost your cool with your child or overreacted. Looking back, how could you have responded differently? Try to make a mental picture of how you would like to respond in the future.

Now take this new mental picture of yourself and continue to rehearse it in your mind. At first, a response such as this may seem unfamiliar and almost impossible; but as you continue setting new patterns

113

in your life, you will see that you can do it. Remember, anger is a natural God-given emotion and is of value when handled in proper ways and at the right times. You must decide how much anger is equal to the crime committed. If you do have a right to be angry, how much anger you should have, and what form will you let it take?

Maybe thinking of anger on a scale of 1-10 might be helpful. *What would anger* act like *if it reached 10 on the scale?* If in your mind, that would be shooting someone, when would you need to do that? In a life or death situation (such as self-defense of you or your family). What would anger at the ten level feel like? "Seeing red," or a total loss of control? How many times in your life have you needed that much anger? Jesus correlated murder and anger in Matthew 5:22, saying that if you are angry with your brother it is akin to murder.

If on the scale, let's say six, is the most anger we would ever be justified in having, and six on the scale means raising your voice, walking away, getting stern, or needing more deliberation on the subject, then this is the pinnacle that our anger should ever reach. Usually this type of anger is more common in marriages in which two people are each trying to be understood rather than seeking to understand. They both feel that the other person is just being stubborn and hardheaded and not at all valuing their position. This can feel tantamount to a slap in the face.

Self-talk and prayer are great ways to stay controlled. By self-talk I mean taking **yourself** aside and telling yourself how you will act and think in provoking situations. You must tell yourself that you refuse to let this or them rob you of your joy. As you are doing this, you can begin to pray and invite the Holy Spirit to help you think properly. Remember, "You can do all things through Christ who gives you strength" (Philippians 4:13). Paul also wrote in Galatians 5:16-17, "**So I say, live by the Spirit, and you will not gratify the desires of the sinful nature. For the sinful nature desires what is contrary to the Spirit, and the Spirit what is contrary to the sinful nature. They are in conflict with each other, so that you do not do what you want.**"

A Christian can be in a negative or unfair situation and still have joy! It really comes down to <u>how one thinks</u> during those times when you have a right to be angry. Don't let yourself get into sin. Deal with it according to the offense, not according to what you may feel. It will come down to choices you make not only to control your emotions, but also the choice of allowing the Holy Spirit to direct you. Today is a great day to start making the changes that will last a lifetime.

CHAPTER SIX

Growing as a Man of God:

THE MENTAL SIDE

"When a country is rebellious, it has many rulers, but a man of understanding and knowledge maintains order"

Proverbs 28:2

Purpose:

To bring structure and profit to the minutes, hours, days, weeks, and years God gives us.

Goal:

To keep peace and run the home and family with as little resistance and as much joy as possible.

Plan:

To have an outline to follow. All members of the family are to be in agreement concerning the outline.

***Key note*:**

This is a guide; not a law! There will be times when we will miss a scheduled and agreed upon assignment. The formula for setting the assignment back in motion is just that: **set it back in motion.**

I want to be able to organize my home and family in a way that is fair and beneficial to everyone involved. This includes what my family expects and needs from me and what I expect and need from them. I must understand what their needs are, and in return, make sure that they know what I'm expecting also.

When something in the home isn't working properly, it is my job as the leader to come up with the solution and share it with my family. I should also ask for the family's input, and then finalize the resolution. This isn't a simple task and *cannot* be taken lightly. However, men, this is your job!

In Ephesians 5:23, it says that **"For the husband is the head of the wife, even as Christ is the head of the Church: and he is the savior of the body."** As Christ leads, protects, directs and provides for the Church, so husbands are to do the same for their wives and families. Let's take a look at the vast area of "working parts" that make up a smooth-operating family.

For men like myself who have children (or even if you don't but one day may want to), we must be aware of what is important to each individual child. My oldest son Michael, is into baseball. It is my job as his dad to make sure that he has everything he needs to play his best. I had my chance at being a ballplayer when I was younger. Now it's his turn, and I must see that he has a fair chance at his dream. For example, I must make sure he gets to practices on time; drive him to the gym to so he can work out; support him as often as possible by being at his games, and listening to his stories on both good days and bad.

My middle child Jonathan is into Martial Arts and video games. As the dad I must be sure that he has his needs met in the same way as Michael. Asking questions like, "How's it going son"? "Do you need anything from dad"? "When is your next event"? One thing I enjoy doing is going to Jonathan's events when they have contact sparring. On one occasion he was paired against a 35 year old man and Jonathan is only 16. Jonathan handled the situation incredibly well and I made sure he heard me tell everyone he had beaten up and older guy. It was God the Father who said in front of a large crowd, "This is my son, whom I love; with him I am well pleased" (Matt 3:17). I guess what I'm saying is, showing genuine interest for the kids because you really care.

Concerning my 11 year old daughter Liana, well she's just into girl stuff! But every night I get to hear all about her day. And, we do all kinds of things together. We go for walks, ride bikes, go out for daddy/daughter breakfasts or lunches, and not only that, but she's been out duck hunting with me a number of occasions and she loves it. They are my children and it is my responsibility to see that they have a dad who is reasonably available and who loves them unconditionally. I must provide food, shelter, care, time, and love for them, as well as, leading them spiritually to know the Lord Jesus Christ.

THE SPIRITUAL ASPECT

Even though we covered most of the spiritual aspects of being a man, let's talk about spiritual things concerning the family. Ideally, the husband is to provide the leadership. He must have his own walk with the Lord in which he is growing in an ever-increasing measure. This is done by having a reasonable amount of time for concentrated Bible reading, a discipline to spend time in prayer, and also by attending church regularly.

The husband is to make room for his wife to develop in her own walk with the Lord. As each of them continues in their spiritual growth, it becomes even more powerful when the two of them walk with Jesus together. The benefits of two people agreeing together in prayer and communing with the Lord has lifelong profitable results and is very powerful. The enemy knows this and seeks to hinder spiritual compatibility. A few ideas for developing together spiritually are: having a family communion time, reading and praying with the children on a regular basis, and the wife and husband serving in a ministry offered in their church.

The Godly husband must live a Christian life that is consistent with the Gospel he preaches. Cursing, drinking, constant fighting, etc., are not good examples to the family, and need to change. Children see right through hypocrisy. We all make mistakes occasionally, but lifestyles that are inconsistent with the Gospel go against producing a spiritually healthy family. Husband, Dad, man of God, change needs to begin with you! You may not see a difference in your spouse right away, but as the leader of the family, it must begin with you.

As we unfold this outline which will greatly aid us in being productive, let me share some godly wisdom with you. As men, we know that our wives are to "submit" to our leadership. However, men, we seem to forget that submission means we also have to answer to *our* commanding officer. We want the women to agree with us and make life easier by doing what we ask, yet we don't want to submit to the things the Lord asks of us. **The wives see this for what it is; a double standard!** When they see us submitting to the Lord, they just might submit to us.

According to author Stu Webber in his book <u>Tender Warrior</u>, the reason we men are "missing it" is, **"We want and expect the women to submit to us being the head; but as men, we don't submit to the headship of the Lord Jesus Christ**." As men, we have been given a "command post" to run our homes, provide for our families, protect and lead them, as well as nurture, sacrifice and love them. We will then have to report back to our commanding officer. How would your report read right now? Would it be poor, just fair, or doing pretty good? How might your wife answer this? (Take a moment and answer this question; let your wife answer it also).

Families come in a variety of sizes and styles. They also grow and evolve as we get older. There are families with newly married couples, families with teenagers, and others with a toddler whose mom is in the workplace. Even still, there are couples who have children which have left the home to go and start their own lives and families. The scenarios can go on and on. The needs of each family will vary, but the fact remains – each family has needs. Your job, as the one who will be reporting to his 'Commanding Officer', is to listen to and detect the needs of each person in the family and do your best to meet them. We must institute a plan that will bring about peace and harmony with the least resistance possible.

Let me say again; if there is a problem in your home, sir, you must come up with a plan! Whether this plan includes asking your wife, asking another man, reading a book, or fasting and prayer (or all of the above), you are responsible for your family. An answer of "**I don't know**" is not acceptable as your "**final answer**". God's promise to you is that He will provide whatever you need. James 1:5 says, "If any of you lack wisdom, let him ask of God, that giveth to all men liberally..."(KJV). Ask it, believe it, receive it!

How Are Your Finances?

I come across so many husbands who do not know how to manage a budget and treat the wife fairly in the area of finances. On the other extreme, there are husbands who completely turn over the responsibility of handling money and the bills to their wives. As men, we must be able to handle our finances in a way that everyone in the family has their individual needs met. So many guys feel it is O.K. to buy a new boat, get season tickets to their favorite sports team, or spend money on what they deem important, and then ignore the needs and desires of the wife and children.

What are the priorities for your family in the area of financial responsibility? Are you tithing? Are you paying the rent or mortgage on time? Is there an adequate food budget? Are the utilities being paid? Does she have a vehicle she can depend on? Is there life insurance in case something were to happen to you? Do the kids have school clothes? Is there room for recreation or entertainment? The list could go on and on. I know how difficult this area is; but with God's help, it is possible to successfully manage your finances. (See the financial section of this book for suggestions).

Debt is something that needs to be addressed and resolved in a timely manner, beginning now! Raising your income or lowering your expenditures are the two basic areas to start. In most cases, the responsibility of providing for the family falls on the husband. *Not handling it is not acceptable.* In many homes today both parents may need to work to meet the demands of family living, and each home must determine what is best for them. It cannot be taken lightly. Have you asked your wife lately how much she needs to run the home in all of its aspects? Guys, don't forget "**walking around**" money if she wants to enjoy a mocha or take a girlfriend to lunch. Sit down and talk with her about your future, the kids' education, vacations, and investments. It is hard work, but well worth it.

A BODY UNDER CONTROL

As you continue progressing up the ladder in your efficiency as a leader, consider your lifestyle in the areas of exercise and diet, as well as any habits that may be ungodly or unhealthy. What shape are you in? The older you get the more difficult it can become to stay in good shape and be physically fit. Keeping a minimal to moderate exercise routine will not only make you feel and look better, but it will give you more energy to accomplish more things.

Diets are difficult to keep and most of the time don't last. May I suggest a complete overhaul in the area of how we eat? A diet really isn't the long term solution; a habit change is. My friend, Dr. Brad Gascoigne, writes in his book Smart Ways to Stay Young and Healthy:

> "The 1991 book, *The Great Divide,* reported that "60 million females and 41 million males are on a diet on an average day!" Obviously, diets alone are seldom the answer. In fact, crash diets and wide fluctuations in body weight are hazardous to your health. Another medical report recently showed that the two factors that helped most with weight loss over long periods of time were *praise* and *exercise.* That is, people who are physically active and are praised for trying to lose weight lose more than do people who are inactive and whose efforts are not acknowledged."

Realize that certain foods that we eat are made to be fattening, and these foods must be seen as a poison. We need a new mindset concerning food consumption. Foods high in fat and calories are for the most part destructive to the human body (for a more detailed outline, see chapter 2, "The Physical Side").

If you are addicted to anything that is destructive to your spiritual, mental, emotional, or physical well-being, you must begin making some changes now. Things like drugs, alcohol, pornography, television, recreation, or amusements, have to be brought under godly submission. This is all part of being a man of God and a leader of your family.

How's Your Anger?

Too many relationships are ruled by emotions that are out of control. As emotions escalate, our ability to say and do the right things are impaired. James 1:19-20 says, "My dear brothers, take note of this: everyone should be quick to listen, slow to speak and slow to become angry, for man's anger does not bring about the righteous life that God desires." Learning to control *what comes out of our mouths* and also *what comes into our minds* is key to successful communication. You might say, "But you don't know how angry she makes me." **No, but I do know how angry you are allowing yourself to get!** Paul told Timothy, "And the Lord's servant must not quarrel; instead, he must be kind to everyone, able to teach, not resentful. Those who oppose him he must *gently* instruct, in the hope that God will grant them repentance leading them to a knowledge of the truth" (2 Timothy 2:24-25).

Controlling how you feel and react is directly related to how you think. You might say, "People are always insulting me and that angers me." You are right. They have no right to do that to you. But are you going to keep letting them control you? The Bible says in Proverbs 12:16 "A fool shows his annoyance at once, but a prudent man overlooks an insult." Being a man who is Spirit and self-controlled is something Christians all have access to because we are children of God (see Romans 8:14-16).

How many of our family problems have been the result of the way we have *handled a problem,* rather than the problem itself? I wonder where they came up with the label "gentlemen?" Guys, we must continually ask the Holy Spirit to help us be gentle and stay gentle. I'm getting better at it myself. To the single men, I want to share some thoughts with you concerning thinking wisely about your life whether you

124

plan on getting married or not. If you're not going to get married, then serve the Lord, stay healthy, make wise choices, save money, and be a good friend. If you plan to get married or remarried, <u>now</u> is the time to develop in each area listed in this book, not later. Maybe one way to look at it is: If your daughter married a man like you, ***what kind of man would she be getting?*** Sobering question, isn't it?

WHAT AREAS DOES MY WIFE NEED HELP IN?

"For as he thinks in his heart, so is he..." (Proverbs 23:7) This sixth area concerning being a man, the mental side, is dealing with how well we think and make choices. Let's look at some practical things that will help our homes be a joyful refuge for everyone who lives there. You may have heard some complaints and frustrations from your wife and may have made feeble attempts to try and rectify some problem areas that continue to arise in your home. However, the problem is still there. There are some things that you will not be able to change overnight, such as a teenager not serving the Lord, or the lack of trust from your wife based on previous choices (or a lack of them). But if you do not evaluate and implement change beginning now, the situation will not get better and may possibly even get worse.

If you were to think back over the majority of your arguments with your wife, what were the issues? In my home, most of our arguments had to do with finances or house cleaning, and occasionally intimacy. Other arguments branched off from there, but the initial complaint was usually one of these topics. I had to come up with a plan to resolve these problem areas.

Each man has to determine the problem areas in his home and with God's help and wisdom, institute a plan which makes life easier. As men, we know that the needs of a wife are different from our own. Finding the *right time* to sit down with our wives and discuss what will make our homes run smoother is important. You may want to start the conversation with something like this: "Honey, I've been thinking about some things that will make our lives a little less stressful. I want to hear from you what you need from me and also what areas you think I may need a little improvement in. I really want to hear what you're saying."

Guys, you will have to brace yourself for what they may say, and you may not even agree with everything, but pre-think your attitude and response. Ask the Lord for wisdom and the right words. You might be pleasantly surprised at the outcome. You might even have a pen and paper with you so she can see that you are serious about what she is saying, and also that you want to be consistent in your efforts.

Yes, it would be easier if the wives simply saw things the way we did, wanted what we wanted, and liked what we liked. But "get real," they don't and won't! 1 Peter 3:7-8 says, **"Husbands, in the same way be considerate as you live with your wives, and treat them with respect as the weaker partner and as heirs with you of the gracious gift of life, so that nothing will hinder your prayers. Finally, all of you, live in harmony with one another; be sympathetic, love as brothers, be compassionate and humble."** This means that I must hear what she has to say and what it is she needs. Once I have an understanding of her needs

126

and wants, I can then determine if I can meet them and how. It requires planning and communication.

An Outline For the Husbands:

Grow in the Lord

It is vitally important that each man continues his development and growth in his walk with Christ. Almost every woman I have ever talked to, if not all of them, deeply desires to see her husband walking closer with Jesus as a way of life. Remember guys, you are the spiritual head of your family. As we covered in Chapter four,
bible reading, prayer, church attendance, and serving in the local church, are all ways to accomplish this.

Pray over family daily

I believe one area all of us men lack in, is, praying enough about our families. Lifting them up before the Father, asking for protection, provision, direction, and wisdom. Almost every time I pray I mention my family members by name to the Lord. Begin to do ths if you haven't started already. You never know what Satan has planned against them for that day, and prayer can short-circuit all of his plans. Let this be a constant for the rest of your life.

Pray with the family

Another practice to implement is learning to pray with your spouse and family as often as possible. I know with the hurried schedules we keep it can be difficult to get everyone together at the same time on a consistent basis, especially as the kids get into their teens. Yet, making sure you are praying as a family is a good thing. Don't forget to pray before each meal and also before important events like school tests, sporting events, and other things such as these. They will appreciate your leadership.

Consistently attend church as a family

Another important factor in leading your family is making sure you are leading them to church. Even if they are somewhat reluctant about going consistently, make sure that you go consistently. If they stop going to church and then you stop going, they are leading you and not the other way around. Show them as a man of God that this is how you live your life. If however, going to church isn't helping you to make positive changes in your life in becoming more Godly, they will see it as hypocrisy. Remember what James 1: 22 says, **"Do not merely listen to the Word and so decieve yourselves. Do what it says"**...

The home is now running smoother because...

Chores

When it comes to household chores (if you're married), does everyone know their job? Having been married now for 20 plus years, I remember how difficult it was and is trying to sort out "stuff" and keep peace in the house. Now I look back and realize how easy it is to accomplish this. The simplicity comes from being relatively organized and having reasonable expectations about how "clean" the house will always be. Let's face it, we live in our homes. It may or may not always be clean. But there are some practical things we can do to make it run smoother. The first question to ask is "Where does my wife need help?" Try not to be overbearing if your wife isn't the neatest person you know. And if she is in a season of being real busy, let's say back in school or demands on the job, be extra sensitive and don't fight about the housecleaning.

Kitchen

Let's begin with the kitchen. Who does the dishes and when? What about random times when they are just sitting in the sink and everyone keeps walking by them but nobody is doing anything about it. If you have children who are old enough to do this job without breaking everything, maybe let them know that on different days you will be asking them to do dishes. Or perhaps, set up a schedule so everyone will know whose turn it is. If the kids aren't old enough yet, sir, where can **you** help your wife? Talk to her and ask her.

Laundry

What about the laundry? I know very few people who get excited about doing laundry. Unfortunately many families let it pile up until it is a mountain of clothes and then nobody wants to do it at all. But it isn't going away on its own. What we need is a plan. It doesn't take much to open the washing machine, put in some laundry soap, throw in the clothes, turn on the machine, close the lid and walk away. When the cycle is over, take the clothes out, open the lid of the dryer, put in the clothes, turn it on and come back later to take them out.

Now someone does have to fold them and then put them away. What we usually do in our house is ask the kids to come and fold their own clothes and then take them to their rooms. Occasionally we will even fold them for them, but they are then responsible to put them away. For me, I have found that doing the colored clothes is real easy. They are usually big things like towels, jeans, shirts, and the like. It's the white clothes that bug me. Things like socks, underwear, and women's items. I know it has to get done so let's talk to her and come up with a system. **What we can't do is keep looking at the pile build up and wish someone would come and take care of it**. Usually, we end up just getting mad that the pile is getting bigger. What's the plan my brother? And remember, if your wife works, she is helping you do your job, so help her do hers. If she doesn't work and isn't keeping the house reasonably clean, taking into consideration the number of kids and their ages of course, have her read my book "The beauty of a Woman".

Dinner

Who is responsible for dinners? Is she the only one to cook? Does she even want you to cook? How often do we bring food home, and when do we eat out? Your budget should dictate some of these issues, but we want to know if your wife needs help and what kind of help. Also, does she have the money she needs for groceries? This is just practical everyday living which each family has to work out. Since you are the leader of your family, you must help come up with a solution.

Garbage and pets

Who takes the garbage out in your house? I know in my house, now that my two sons are teenagers, the garbage issue is much easier. I still take it out occassionally just because it's not a big deal, but usually I say, "Hey Mike or Johnny, please take out the garbage", and it gets done. Is this a source of contention in your house? What is the rule for the kids keeping their rooms tidy and neat? My counsel would be not to stress too much about it, however, there should be a reasonable amount of regular 'clean ups' in their rooms. And what about the family pets? Pets are another great way of teaching responsibilty to children. Keeping the pets fed, having fresh water, picking up after their mess, all of these are positive training to help the kids learn responsibilty.

Kids' homework

As our three kids continue to grow and mature, the homework situation has gotten easier, at least in the category of them getting it done. Each child, Michael, Jonathan, and Liana, has established a routine for getting their assignments completed. Let me interject right here that, each of them are completely different in their personality, desire, and ability when it comes to schoolwork. Jonathan, our middle child, never has to be prodded to do his work. He just understands that it has to be done, so he gets it done. Michael on the other hand, takes the path of least resistence. Because he was our first child, every time we asked him if he had finished his homework he would say yes. We just assumed that he had. When he started turning in a few bad grades we realized that he hadn't. So with Liana, who is more like Michael, we have to stay on top her homework. It is arduous at times, to say the least. But, it is our responsibility as the parents to make sure it gets done. And it is your responsiblity as the parents to see that your children are getting their homework done. It is the job of both parents.

"To do" list

One last thing; the honey-do list. I know **'the list'** can be overwhelming and cause feelings of frustration which can lead to arguments, but at some point, in a reasonable amount of time, the list must get done, that is if you want peace in your house. Ask your wife to write them down in her order of importance and then give her an approximate time when she can expect them done. In some cases you may have to hire someone who has the time and skill to do a specific job, but you can't just do nothing about it. Do the things you can, the things you like and the things you have time for. Hire out the rest. Usually there is someone at church who can help or at least knows someone who can get it done. You can do it my brother!

Kids' chores

I believe it is vitally important that kids have family chores they are responsible to do. The older they get the more they must see that soon they will be doing life on their own. They must learn responsibilty. Remember dad, we only have them for so long and then we turn them loose to face a hostile world. Our job as parents is make sure they are ready to face the rigors of life. Calmly institute structure with some possible positive affirmations, such as, an allowance for doing chores thoroughly and the way you have asked them to be done, or possibly buying something they would like because you see their effort and relatively good attitude. Use wisdom and let the Lord and other successful dads give you some thoughts on this.

Finances

Family grocery and household needs. How much per week or month do you need to pay the bills? If delegating to your wife, make sure that she knows how much she is getting and when she is getting it (See chapter 3, FINANCIAL STABILITY & GROWTH). The bottom line is, you must make sure the financial needs of your family are met. All of them!

Schedules

Does your wife know your weekly schedule, or is she often surprised? (How about a family calendar where everyone can see it?) Does she agree with the priority structure of your scheduling (the when, what, and why of your schedule)? How do you handle when the kids are sick and have to miss school, or what about soccer or baseball schedules? All of these must be dicussed.

Understanding your wife's needs

Does she have a break time? As men, we must understand the strain our wives are under. Not only do they take care of the children but they also take care of the home and many of them have jobs outside of the home. They too need a break, an opportunity to "let their hair down," spend some time with a girlfriend having lunch or going to a movie. When is a reasonable time for her to go out? How often? Once a week, every two weeks, once a month? The best thing you can do for her is to bring this up and ask her. Don't just think this sounds like a good and fair idea, put it into motion by bringing it up to her. When it comes to groceries, occasionally extra needs may arise. What we encourage the wives to do is, communicate beforehand to your husband what the extra need may be, so as not to catch him off guard. Try to not mention it at the last minute in a frustrated manner.

Her job

If your wife works, she cannot be the sole "housekeeper." She will need your support in almost all areas in taking care of the home and children. And don't forget about the fatique factor. I hear men often say to me, "I'm tired too". Yes, I know. But the Bible says she is the physically weaker vessel. Men you have to step up and carry the extra weight. That's just the way it is.

For the Wives:

Understanding your husband's needs
(Maybe have your wife read this section with you.)

To support her husband in love, life, home, work, ministry, recreation, and the demands of his job. This will require mercy and flexibility as she fulfills her role as helpmate. She must understand that he has worked all day also. Most men I talk with comment on how important it is for them to be greeted with a friendly attitude when they arrive home from work, and also how nice it is to see the house in a relatively decent order.

Romance
During a recent survey taken at our church, 99.9% of the men said that they loved their wife, found her attractive, and desired her sexually. I cannot overemphasize how important having a good intimate relationship is to a man. Ladies, if you struggle with sexual intimacy with your husband, please talk to an older woman who has wisdom in this area. If

need be, see a counselor, or at least the pastor's wife. However, your struggle may be from your husband's attitude, behavior, or technique. If so, find the right time to try and communicate with him your desires and needs. If communicating this doesn't bring a change find someone he feels comfortable talking with for counsel. (Be sensitive in your approach; you know, male ego and all).

But ladies, please understand how important this is to most men. Your husband is supposed to desire you all the time. He's supposed to be captivated by your beauty. From the women I've talked to, it's really not sexual intimacy that is the root problem but rather the way they are treated from day to day. Then, right before bedtime the husband suddenly turns "nice". Guys, my question is, "Why aren't you treating her nice all the time anyway?" Hey, the bottom line is, if you want more sex, guys, try treating her like a queen everyday and maybe you might become the "King" of the bedroom!

Finances

It is important for the wife not only to **understand** the working of the family finances, but also to help **keep** the family budget (by staying within the budget concerning credit cards, ATM cards, checks, etc.). Reading the financial section of this book should shed some light on the family budget and budgeting. Finances must be handled as a team. Both the husband and wife must stick to the budget. If one or the other violates the budget, this could cause negative "feelings" and may start an argument. If so, see chapter 5, The Emotional Side.

Recreation and relaxation

When the wife is understanding concerning the recreational needs of the husband as an outlet from the pressures of providing, leading and directing the family, this brings a sense of relaxation for the man. If, when he asks about taking a break once in a while, he is consistently met with opposition, this just adds to the daily frustration of life. Here are some questions to ask concerning recreation:

1) How often *can he* indulge in recreation? 2) Can we afford it? 3) Are the priorities of the family being met concerning finances and time spent with the wife, kids, church, etc.? Each husband must check his priorities and motives. Psalms 4:4 says, **"In your anger do not sin; when you are on your beds, search your hearts and be silent."** Again in Psalms 32:8, **"I will instruct you and teach you in the way you should go; I will counsel you and watch over you."** Finally in Psalms 139:23-24, **"Search me, O God, and know my heart; test me and know my anxious thoughts. See if there is any offensive way in me, and lead me in the way everlasting."**

As you begin implementing these principles you will feel a sense of accomplishment and positive pride. Remember, God is on your side and "I can do everything through Him who gives me strength." (Philippians 4:13)

Together you are a team! Enjoy your life! God has great things in store for you!

OLD TESTAMENT REFERENCES
(In Biblical Reference Order)

Genesis 4:1-7
Genesis 34
Genesis 39
Genesis 49:5-7

1 Samuel 17:28-29
1 Samuel 20:33

2 Samuel 11
2 Samuel 11:6
2 Samuel 11:9
2 Samuel 11:13
2 Samuel 12:8

1 Kings 1:1-6
1 Kings 2:2-3

Joshua 14:6-11

Job 1:1
Job 31:1

Psalm 4:4
Psalm 6:1
Psalm 19:7-14
Psalm 32:8
Psalm 37:4
Psalm 37:21
Psalm 38:1
Psalm 103:1-7
Psalm 139:23-24

Proverbs 3:9-10
Proverbs 3:28
Proverbs 4:20-22
Proverbs 6:6
Proverbs 7:22-27
Proverbs 10:4-5
Proverbs 11:1
Proverbs 11:24-25
Proverbs 12:1
Proverbs 12:13

Proverbs 12:16
Proverbs 13:11
Proverbs 13:22
Proverbs 14:23
Proverbs 14:31
Proverbs 15:27
Proverbs 16:2
Proverbs 17:10
Proverbs 17:16
Proverbs 18:9
Proverbs 18:22
Proverbs 19:3
Proverbs 19:10
Proverbs 19:14
Proverbs 19:17
Proverbs 20:4
Proverbs 20:13
Proverbs 20:17
Proverbs 20:23
Proverbs 21:6
Proverbs 21:17
Proverbs 21:20
Proverbs 22:1
Proverbs 22:7
Proverbs 22:16
Proverbs 22:22-23
Proverbs 22:24-25
Proverbs 22:26-27
Proverbs 23:4-5
Proverbs 23:7
Proverbs 24:11-12
Proverbs 24:30-34
Proverbs 25:28
Proverbs 27:4
Proverbs 27:9
Proverbs 27:17
Proverbs 27:23-27
Proverbs 28:19

Proverbs 29:25
Proverbs 30:7-8
Proverbs 31:30

Ecclesiastes 4:9

Jeremiah 5:8

Ezekiel 33:1-9

Malachi 3:8-12

NEW TESTAMENT REFERENCES
(In Biblical Reference Order)

Matthew 5:7
Matthew 5:22
Matthew 5:28
Matthew 6:33
Matthew 13:22
Matthew 21:12-13
Matthew 22:21
Matthew 25:14-30
Matthew 26:41

Mark 11:15-17

Luke 4:18
Luke 19:45-46

John 2:13-17
John 14:15
John 15:10-11

Acts 2:36-38
Acts 10:1-48
Acts 26:18

Romans 6:11-14
Romans 8:9,14
Romans 8:10
Romans 8:14-16
Romans 10:9-10
Romans 12:1

Romans 12:3
Romans 12:19
Romans 13:7
Romans 13:8
Romans 15:14

1 Corinthians 2:9-12
1 Corinthians 2:10-16
1 Corinthians 6:9-10
1 Corinthians 6:19
1 Corinthians 7:2-3
1 Corinthians 10:13-14

2 Corinthians 9:6-11

Galatians 2:11-13
Galatians 3:26
Galatians 5:16-17
Galatians 5:19-21
Galatians 5:22-23
Galatians 6:2

Ephesians 2:2
Ephesians 2:8
Ephesians 2:14
Ephesians 4:20
Ephesians 4:24
Ephesians 4:26
Ephesians 5:18

Ephesians 5:23
Ephesians 6:4
Ephesians 6:7

Philippians 1:6
Philippians 2:4
Philippians 4:6-8
Philippians 4:8-9
Philippians 4:13
Philippians 4:19

Colossians 2:3

1 Thessalonians 4:3-7

2 Thessalonians 3:6-15

1 Timothy 1:19
1 Timothy 4:8
1 Timothy 5:2
1 Timothy 5:8
1 Timothy 6:9-10

2 Timothy 1:7
2 Timothy 2:4
2 Timothy 2:24-25

Titus 1:15
Titus 2:3

Hebrews 12:1-2

James 1:5
James 1:13-15
James 1:20
James 3:1
James 3:17-18
James 4:2
James 5:16
James 5:20

1 Peter 1:22
1 Peter 2:2
1 Peter 3:7-8

2 Peter 1:5

1 John 4:10

Notes

Quotes from this book come from the New International Version (NIV) of the Bible.

1First Place, More information can be found out about this program at www.firstplace.org

1Covey, Stephen, Principle Centered Leadership, Simon & Schuster, 1992

1Gascoigne, Dr. Bradley, Smart Ways to Stay Young and Healthy, Ronin Publishing, Inc., 1992, p. 22

1Clayson, George, The Richest Man in Babylon, New American Liberty Trade, 1991

1MacArthur, John, The MacArthur New Testament Commentary, Ephesians, 1986, Moody Press, p. 152

1Gascoigne, Dr. Bradley, Smart Ways to Stay Young and Healthy, Ronin Publishing, Inc., 1992, p. 33

1Weber, Stu, Tender Warrior: God's Intention for a Man, Multnomah Publishers Inc., 1999